Through the Fire

THERESA A. VANDERMEER

Publication date February 2017

ISBN Print: 978-1520780801

1. Fire 2. Death 3. Surgeries 4. Rehabilitation 5. Prayer

6. Rehab 7. Hope

Through the Fire may be purchased at special quantity discounts for burn related nonprofits, fundraising, book clubs, or educational purposes for churches, schools and universities. For more information or to have Theresa speak at your event: throughthefirebytheresa@gmail.com

Cover, Layout, Design: Theresa A. Vandermeer

Publisher: Theresa A. Vandermeer

Printed in the United States of America

This book is dedicated to the beholden memory of Lawrence Clifford Roberts, who gave his life for mine

&

To the Vandermeer's – Mom & Dad – who answered God's calling to be my adoptive parents, not born of their womb but from their hearts!

THROUGH THE FIRE

Table of Contents

Acknowledgements

You were there in the beginning of my memories as I cradled you, protected and comforted you – my only sanity in the midst of chaos. Over the years, much like a beautiful butterfly, your scattered presence landed in my life many times, but only long enough to remind me that you were still there and to keep hanging on for better tomorrows. Today, it is your permanent presence and our intuitive twin nature that not only makes us great sisters, but the best of friends. Thank you Karen for loving me through it all - the good, the bad, and the ugly.

The Night Before the Tragedy

My story begins the night before the tragedy. It had been a long night. Everyone was drinking again - Mom, Dad, my older sister Linda, and Uncle Carl. I was so tired as I looked at everyone passed out on the floor and the front porch. It was late, and I was too scared to go lie down with my baby sister Karen in the dark bedroom, which was off to the right of the living room.

Uncle Carl, who was my Mama's oldest brother, had told me that a man had been shot in that room and that his ghost was still roaming there. Uncle Carl was a lighthearted man and a jokester, so I never knew if he was playing around or not, but there were stains on the floor as proof so I believed what he said. Karen was crying from hunger, and her diaper was soaking wet. She had just had her second birthday, and I was almost five years old. I remember many nights just like this one - feeling tired, hungry, scared, and alone without parental care. It was because of nights like this one that I was forced to grow up very fast and take care of my little sister and myself. Knowing what I had to do, I stood at the bedroom door peering into the dark inside.

I knew that if I could just run and jump onto bed and hide under the covers, everything would be okay. The ghost would not hurt me. Just like on the other nights, as I stood there contemplating for what seemed like forever, I finally gathered enough courage and strength inside me for action. I reached down, grabbed my little sister's hand, and we ran into the room. Frantically, I pushed her up onto the bed and quickly hid under the covers with her. I remember many nights lying there beside my baby sister, listening to the laughter, fighting, and screaming going on outside my uncle's bedroom because everyone was drinking.

Mama told me she lost her first four children to the Department of Social Services. Of course, I did not understand this. Mama was a good hearted person. She was very kind and she was very sweet. She really loved us girls and she told us that all the time, but she continually got caught up in her world of partying and she let it ruin her life and ours. I hated the drinking. Often, they would stay drunk for days and just lie around on the couch, on the floor, or on the outside steps. Because of all this, I was forced to take care of myself and my baby sister Karen, and there were many times that we went hungry and un-bathed. I remember one occasion where my older sister Linda, who was drunk, got in a fight with Dad. She threw a rock at him, but it missed him and hit my baby sister in the head. I was crying when I saw her head bleeding profusely. I was scared! She had to be taken to the emergency room to get stitches. She still has a scar from it today.

Other times the fighting got so bad that we would walk barefoot up the long dirt road to the end of the holler and knock on the door of an elderly neighbor. I remember telling this old lady lies to avoid the truth that Mom and Dad were drinking and fighting. Somehow she knew that we needed her. She became our friend and angel in times like these. She always sat us down at the kitchen table, giving us treats of Fig Newtons and milk. I didn't really like Fig Newtons at that time, but I ate them because I was so hungry and so thankful to have something to eat.

Life for me was crazy and unpredictable. Although we were staying at Uncle Carl's house, I don't remember ever having a place to live or call our own. Because of all the fighting and drinking, we were constantly evicted from our homes. Many times we would wait until dark and sneak up under the West Gate Bridge in West Asheville to sleep. However, I remember that when Mama was sober, she cooked biscuits and gravy for us, or we went to soup kitchens to eat.

Walking barefoot was a common practice for Karen and me. I don't remember ever owning a pair of new shoes. Christmas wasn't a holiday that I even knew. Eating mud pies with my baby sister and Crabapples from my Uncle's backyard is something that I remember well. I would get worms from them, and Mama would treat them with chewing tobacco. Partying, drinking, and fighting were things that I knew well. This may seem shocking, but I even would occasionally drink and stick my head in a brown paper bag to sniff glue. Children tend to imitate adults.

It was the end of April, and the weather had warmed. Karen and I spent most of our waking hours outside playing in the dirt by an old apple tree. I loved the feel of the fresh green grass under my bare feet as I ran all around with little or no parental supervision. Sometime that afternoon, we heard Mama and Uncle

Carl yelling at each other. We were staying with him because we had nowhere else to go, but Uncle Carl told Mama we needed to leave right away. He said Mama needed to get a job and get her own place.

I have many memories of moving around a lot during my early childhood. We went to Florida and picked oranges. We stayed at my aunt's subsidized apartment in West Asheville and spent nights under bridges near West Gate to give a few examples. I don't remember ever having my own room or toys to play with. Home to me was being with Mama and Karen.

Mama was yelling for us to go to Uncle Clifford's, who lived in the country in Weaverville. She said he had a surprise for us. Excited, we kissed Uncle Carl goodbye and jumped in the car. Lucille, my Aunt, was there to pick us up and drive us to Uncle Clifford's home. Uncle Clifford was Mama's older brother. He was a very kindhearted, generous man who lived a very simple lifestyle and although he did not have room for us in his home, he agreed to let us stay there until Mama found somewhere else to go. I really didn't know Clifford well, but the few times I saw him in my early childhood I remembered him as having had a very comforting smile and kind heart. Riding in the car to his house, this time I couldn't help feeling excited as I anticipated what his surprise could possibly be!

"A red tricycle" I screamed as I jumped out of the car, pulling Karen beside me.

"You'll have to share it," Uncle Clifford said as he gave us a big hug. Us was Karen; cousins Brenda and Joyce, who were visiting; and me. I had never ridden a tricycle before, but I caught on fast. The afternoon flew by, and I soon found myself waving good-bye to my cousins. Dad and Uncle Carl started the grill, and we had hamburgers for dinner that night.

The afternoon quickly turned into night, and I found myself crawling up onto my uncle's empty bed. He lived in a one-bedroom house, and the furnishings were very plain just like the old mattress that my sister and I laid down on which had no sheets on it. Worn out from the excitement of the day, without a hug or a kiss or knowing where Mama was, I closed my eyes, happy from the fun of the day and relieved to be out of the other house with the ghost in it. Not knowing any different; everything in my world seemed perfect that day, thinking about riding the red tricycle again in the morning. I had no idea as I closed my heavy eyelids that life as I now knew it was going to change forever.

For most people, it was just a normal day; however, it was the day that would change my life forever. The person I knew - that cute little blonde-haired, blue-eyed, rosy-cheeked little girl named Teresa Ann Lundy - would be no more.

Teresa Ann Lundy before fire, age four

(Artwork drawn by Miriam Vandermeer)

*Teresa and her two sisters, Linda and Karen (left)
Teresa and cousin Kenny (right)*

*Teresa (in pink), and her cousins
before the fire.*

Consumed by Fire

After what seemed like only a few moments of sleep, I was woken up by piercing screams. At first, I thought I had woken up from a nightmare; however, very quickly I realized the bad dream was actually my reality—the house was on fire! Panic filled my entire being as I gasped for fresh air. Frozen in fear, I quickly realized that I was all alone. Tears began to pour down my face as the flames, which roared through the darkness of the night, seemed to dance and beckon to me with human-like arms. Faint screams that were not my own carried through the roaring flames as shadows passed outside the nearby window. My blurry, tear-filled eyes stung from the heat and smoke as I panicked to find the door in my mind. My tears quickly turned into intense heart-felt gasps of crying as I realized that my left foot was stuck in the springs of the old sheet-less mattress, which had a hole in it.

Drenched in sweat from the pain I was already feeling from the intense heat, I screamed out for my Mama as I frantically twisted my foot to try to get free. All I could think of was where was she and why had she left me here all alone? The flames quickly came closer as they surrounded the bed where I lay. My skin began to physically melt off of me as I felt my body growing weaker from the heat and the short sporadic shallow breaths I was barely able to take. With each gasp of smoky air, I felt my inner struggle begin to fade as I feared that I may never get out alive.

In the midst of a moment of sudden peace when I had given up the fight for life, a dark shadow suddenly came running toward me through the roaring flames with piercing screams and outstretched arms as he called out my name, "Teresa!" I couldn't see clearly, but I recognized this person by the tone of his voice. It was Uncle Clifford. He had come to save me! Within seconds, he had my left foot unstuck from the springs as he picked me up in his strong arms and ran me to the nearby window. With a whisper of "I love you" in my ear and a kiss on my head, he quickly lifted me up and pushed me out to my Mama, who was anxiously screaming my name and reaching for me from the outside.

When Mama touched me, I cried out in pain as more of my skin rolled off of my arms. Trying to adjust my eyesight in the darkness of the night, I quickly realized that I could not see. My eyes were already swollen shut from the burns on my face. By this time, Mama heard the sound of an ambulance and grabbed both Karen and me, tucked us both up under each arm, and started running toward the top of the dirt road. Halfway there, tired from exhaustion, she tried to put me down to see if I could walk, but I screamed out, "Mama, I can't see!" Mama began crying and yelling out loud, "Oh God, please don't let her die!"

At that very moment, with child-like assurance in my voice, I grabbed her leg and said, "Mama, I'm not going to die." Somehow I knew in my heart at that very moment that my life was not over and that I was going to make it for her. I was not going to give up! After all, Uncle Clifford had saved me from the roaring flames! I could not let him down.

At the top of the hill, we met the rescue squad. When the man took me from my mother's arms, I screamed in excruciating pain as he laid me down on the stretcher. At that point, the last thing I can remember before losing consciousness was asking the man beside me why he was cutting off my clothes - at least the parts that were not gone or stuck to my already melted skin.

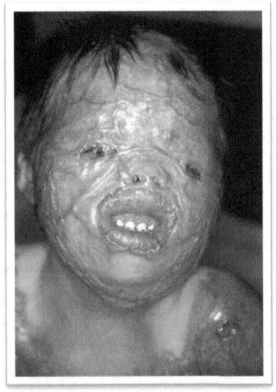

Four months after house fire, 1976

Why Me?

I cried out for you, Mama,
But you were nowhere to be seen.
My eyes were filled with tears and smoke
As I called out your name
I was left all alone as the flames beckoned to me,
Oh God, please, why me?
The flames overtook, me and they would not let go
As they took away my skin, my beauty,
My hair, my fingers, and my clothes
They even tried to take my very own soul
But I would not let them
I just could not let go!

The Fight Begins

I arrived at Memorial Mission Hospital by ambulance, approximately half an hour after the house had caught fire, according to my hospital records. They showed that due to the extreme pain that I was in, and the loss of body fluids from the amount of burns that I had received, that I had completely become unconscious shortly after being put on the stretcher at the scene of the fire. The rescue team, per protocol, also had to heavily sedate me with pain medication due to the severity of my burns.

At Mission Hospital, my condition was considered extremely critical, because I had suffered from 65 percent total body burns with 43 percent being the worst—third degree. My records also showed that there was significant swelling in the back of my throat from the smoke that I had inhaled and that my head was extremely swollen from the burns. My fingers were charcoal black, and most of my hair and facial features had been burned off to the point where I was unrecognizable. That night, in my fight for life in the emergency room, my vitals failed three different times, and I had to be resuscitated back to life.

The first critical treatment took place while I was at Memorial Mission Hospital, which consisted of scraping off the black, dead skin from both of my arms. This procedure is called wound dermal debridement and it is a necessary treatment used on newly burned patients; it removes dead flesh from their body in order to promote healing. This is a procedure that I underwent many times over the next couple of months. It is supposed to not only promote healing but to also help reduce scarring. I have no recollection of this being done at this time because of the heavy pain medication that I was on, but I do later on down the road.

On April 27, 1976, three days after the fire, I was flown to the Shriners Burn Center in Cincinnati, Ohio, on a private airplane by the Shriners Network. This hospital is one of twenty-two nonprofit medical facilities run by the Shriners. Their agency helps children with burns receive medical care in a family-centered environment, regardless of their family's ability to pay. It is here at this particular hospital that my road to recovery began.

Over the next few months, my hospitalization stay here consisted of numerous surgeries, which included skin grafting, finger amputations, and wound debridement of my face, arms, legs, back, and chest. Because I had lost so much fluid and blood from my burns, I was transfused with 14 units of whole blood during my acute stay.

Mama was put in Memorial Mission Hospital for one week back in Asheville, North Carolina, for second degree burns on her face, arms, and back. Karen had made it out of the fire with just one small burn on her hand. After Mama was released from the hospital, she was flown up to Cincinnati by the Shriners, who gave her room and board at the Ronald McDonald's House.

I don't know exactly how long it was before I

regained consciousness from the heavy medication I was on, but when I awoke, there were millions of questions that ran through my head. The first one was, why couldn't I see? And the second, why was I so cold? Apparently, I kept fading in and out of consciousness for weeks.

Mama said that they kept telling her that they did not know if I would make it. She said that every time she asked the doctors, they kept telling her that my condition was poor and that there didn't seem to be a lot of hope. I kept getting infection after infection, which had to be fought off with antibiotics, and the fingers on my right hand had to be removed one by one as they slowly died. My left foot, which had gotten caught in the springs of the mattress, was badly burned; and at one point, they thought they might have to amputate it as well due to severe infection. Mama said that I developed a staph infection, which got into my bloodstream, and I kept running a fever and had to be put on an airbed with ice packs. She said that I jerked and trembled constantly from the fever and pain, but thankfully, my body was able to fight it off with the assistance of IV antibiotics.

My eyes were sewn shut for six weeks because of fear of infection causing blindness. I could not eat regular food and had to eat the soup Mama fed me through a straw. Mama said that she tried to sneak me a few potato chips from time to time; she would crush them up really small, but I always choked on them. Mama read me many stories and stayed with me as much as they allowed her to for a few weeks. On many occasions, I asked her where Karen, Dad, and Uncle Clifford were and why they had not come to visit me. I especially missed Karen, and my heart feared that she was all alone, not being fed, changed, or taken care of. I did not understand why she couldn't come to visit me. I wanted to make sure she was okay. Mama always just told me that everyone was fine, and that they could not fly all the way up to Cincinnati to see me, but that they loved me very much. She told me that she had to lie to me about my Uncle Clifford. She said that she was too scared at that time to tell me the truth because she was afraid that I would go into shock. She said the therapist had advised her to wait as well. It was not till sometime later when I became physically stable, that I learned that Clifford had been my angel here on earth. I was told that after he pushed me out of the window to my Mama the night of the fire, that his house immediately collapsed in on him. The remains of his body were found hours later when they had completely put out the fire. He had given up his life to save mine.

Asheville Man, 39, Dies In Reems Creek Area Fire

(Asheville Citizen Times Newspaper Article)

"Lawrence Clifford Roberts, 39, died late Friday night in a fire which also injured his sister and her two children, the Buncombe County Sheriff's Department reported. A spokesman at Memorial Mission Hospital reported Saturday night that the sister, Mrs. Ella Mae Lundy, 33, of the same address, was in satisfactory condition with second degree burns over 3% of her body. Her daughter Teresa, four, was listed in critical condition in the pediatrics intensive care unit with third degree burns over 65% of her body, the spokesman said. Another daughter, Karen, was injured but not hospitalized. The fire was in a house on Union Chapel Road off Reems Creek Road. According to Chief Zina Cole of the Reems Creek Volunteer Fire Department, the fire was reported about 11:30 PM by a neighbor who saw the glow. The roof already had fallen in when firemen arrived. Mrs. Lundy, who had brought the two children out to the road, told the firemen there was still someone in the burning house, but she was too upset to tell them who or how many. The fire was put out in about an hour, after which Robert's body was found in the charred ruins. Mrs. Lundy told investigators that Robert's ran into the house to save her little girl Teresa. Thirty to forty firemen half from the Reem's Creek Fire Department and half from the Weaverville Fire Department fought the fire. A Reems Creek ambulance and a Buncombe County ambulance transported the injured to the hospital."

16

There is no record of an investigation ever being done; however, my mother Ella Mae told me that my father, Sammy, had had "a bad run-in" with a friend of his and that this friend set the house on fire to get back at him. The man who did it thought that Sammy was in the house at the time he set the house on fire. The man who did it also had just gotten out of prison the day before. I never saw my father that night. He had fled the scene long before the ambulance or the cops arrived. The house fire was not an accident.

A Glimmer of Hope

My stay in the hospital lasted three long months, during which time I underwent numerous surgeries that involved getting many skin grafts. Some grafts took, and others didn't, so they had to wait to do more. Because there were so many open areas on my body that needed skin grafts, the process was slow. They had to wait for areas of my skin that had already been used before for grafting to heal so that they could reuse another piece of skin from that same area for a new graft. Because the majority of the burns on my body were second – and third-degree burns, my original skin could not rejuvenate on its own. The skin plays such an important function in our body. It helps our body regulate temperature, it gives us sensory perception, it excretes important chemicals from our body through sweating, and it helps with metabolic functions such as the formation of vitamin D, to mention a few.

Although the doctors try hard to restore these important functions in our body, the resilience and elasticity of our normal skin can never be recovered. That is why even with the best care, second- and third-degree burn scarring still occurs. Because the amount of grafts that I needed was limited, the doctors had to use other temporary methods to help keep my raw open burned areas covered. The temporary process that was used on me was pig skin - which was used to provide temporary wound coverage or wound closure for my burns. The skin was also used to protect me from getting wound infections from the loss of body fluids. It was not actually incorporated into my own skin, but it served as a temporary substitute until my own skin healed so that they could put new grafts over the burned areas.

The process was a very strange experience for me. Not only did the pig skin have a terrible odor because of what was used to preserve it, but it was a foreign thing that was temporarily laid over large areas of my body every day. For the first few months, I had to have dressing changes done twice a day with the use of the pig skin to prevent infections. During the dressing changes, they would scrape off any dead skin, cover the area with new pig skin, apply Silvadene cream to the area, and re-dress it with new bandaging. The pain I remember from having the bandages put on and off was excruciating. The oozing from my burns was continuous and leaked through my bandages. When it came time to change them, they would stick to my skin. I remember the nurses having to soak the dried, crusted areas in warm water in order to get them off so they would not rip off the scabs or any new skin that may have begun to grow.

Later down the road, when I became more stable and mobile, they began to put me in a whirlpool bath filled with iodine to help loosen the bandages on my body and to help fight infections. This was a routine that I had to undergo several times a day.

The days and nights seemed so long. One minute I was awake and alert, and the next I was being transported off to surgery, anxious and sick. One minute I was feeling calm, and the next, I was feeling jittery, scared, and full of pain. Frustration and uncertainty filled my whole being. However, a small glimmer of hope came into my life when I began to see spots of yellow through the bandages that were over my eyes. What was once darkness was now filled with glimpses of yellow light which I clung to throughout my waking hours. I remember fighting with myself to not go to sleep in case that glimpse of light would fade away.

Where is the Real Me?

Six weeks passed by, and the bandages from my eyes were finally removed. For the first time in what seemed like forever, I was able to see again; and the surroundings that I had only guessed about now became a blurred reality to me.

There beside me stood several people that I did not know but with voices that I recognized from the darkness. By this time, Mama's visits had ended. Deep inside my heart, I had hoped that she would have been there to surprise me when they took the bandages off my eyes, but she was nowhere to be seen among the strangers' eyes that now glared at me. I don't remember how long she actually stayed with me in the hospital because the days and nights all blurred together, but years later, she explained to me that she could not handle seeing me go through the pain, especially not knowing if I would make it, so she had to emotionally detach herself. I guess her running away was the only way she knew how to deal with the awful uncertainty of her burned child.

What I remember feeling after my blurry eyes were able to focus was total dismay and sadness. I can recall the shock that I experienced when I looked down under the open arch at my arms, legs, and hands. What I saw was a foreign naked body with large red square patches of skin and bandages everywhere that was not mine! Overwhelming bursts of uncontrollable tears streamed down my face as I looked at myself, and a million questions ran through my mind. Were these really my arms and hands? Was this really my body? Who had hurt me this way? Why did I not have my fingers anymore? I knew that the nurses had told me that I had been burned, but how did I know what burned looked like? Was this really me? All I wanted to do was run and scream, but I could not move. I felt so numb, helpless, and weak. I felt as though I was put into a different body, and it was one that I did not like at all. It scared me. I scared myself. I was different from the person I once knew. I was ugly. What happened to Mama's beautiful little girl? Who was she now?

At this point, I remember someone stepping close to me and holding a hand-held mirror toward me, asking me if I wanted to see my face. With a blank stare and a hesitant nod yes from me, she slowly held it up toward my face. The moment my eyes caught the first glimpse of my face, I gasped. I felt as though my heart almost leaped out of my chest. I can't even begin to express the overwhelming feelings I felt at this point. I was looking at someone, or something, that was not me! I wanted to rip the scars, this mask off my face. I wanted to see me. I wanted to see Teresa - the real me! What had I done to deserve this punishment?

All I remember doing is shaking my head back and forth and screaming, "I want out! Let me out! Please get me out of here!"

Several people tried to talk to me and calm me down, but I could not hear what they were saying in the midst of my own screaming. Not being able to quickly console me, they had to give me medication to calm me down. The last thing I remember is several hands reaching out, grabbing my body, and giving me a shot as I quickly faded back into the darkness.

Whispers from Jesus

With Mama being gone now for some time, my heart was heavy with sadness. All that I could think about was being back home and playing with my baby sister. I was so worried about her and wondered if she was being properly taken care of. Although my days were filled with surgeries, dressing changes, medication dosages, and whirlpool baths, they seemed so long and empty without her there by my side. Mama was not there to read to me, help me drink my soup through a straw, or talk to me and encourage me through the day. Instead, all I heard were the sounds of nurses' voices at the nursing station, the beeping of the IV machines, and an occasional TV show that I might have tuned into that was hanging on the wall, unable to change the channel myself.

The silence drove me crazy. I spent much time lying in my room trapped on the air bed, unable to move without assistance, staring at the bare walls. I had to lie on an air bed because I had over 65% of my body burned. Severe burns (second and third degree) like mine can cause bed sores; therefore, they used an air bed to provide me with comfort and to help prevent me from getting bed sores. It also helped ensure that my skin was kept dry in a comfortable and controlled air atmosphere. The air was supposed to be warm but laying there I felt very cold. A metal casing was placed over my body from neck to feet on the air bed and then a sheet was draped over it. This was to prevent anything from touching and sticking to my open wounds so that they could dry out quicker. So the picture I saw in front of me at all times when I looked downward was my naked foreign body covered in bandages.

However, in the midst of my sadness, pain and overwhelming confusion, I can remember lying there on that air bed, with cold air blowing all around me, and feeling as if someone was there beside me, holding my hand. Was it because I wanted my Mama to be there so bad that I felt as though she was or was someone else really there with me? A warm presence, a comforter, a friend... someone was there!

Every day this presence stayed with me, as though they were standing right beside my bed; and for some reason, I no longer felt as alone. It was as if someone was whispering in my ear words of encouragement and equipping my soul with this incredible will to fight, to live! Each day I began to feel a renewed inner strength, a constant whispering as though someone was lifting my spirit and breathing in me this incredible, overwhelming desire to fight the battle that was set before me.

Over time thoughts of sadness began to turn into joy as my physical strength and child-like attitude re-emerged. Every day I began the process of familiarizing and connecting my spirit with my new image, which I constantly stared at through the reflection of the silver side rails on the hospital bed. Although my bright-red blistered skin and useless hands looked like foreign objects to me, I soon began to accept them as my own - as part of the new Teresa that I had now become.

Days turned into weeks, and I was soon allowed to

get up out of bed and ride around in a wheelchair. Because my right foot had been burned so severely to where I almost had to have it amputated, I was not able to walk on it at this point. It too had been grafted, and a special splint had been put on it to help prevent contractures. At this point, I remember spending most of my time on the laps of the nurses at the nurses' station. It being a burn center, I quickly discovered that I was not the only one who had been "hurt" this way. There were other kids my age, and even little babies. Even though they were like me in many ways, I still was afraid to look at them. They mirrored me and were a constant reminder of my own burns. When their eyes met mine, my soul wanted to cry. In the world I once knew, I had never been surrounded by so many hurt people. It now was becoming a norm that I did not like. My heart always felt this overwhelming heavy sadness every time I looked at someone new because I knew exactly how they were feeling inside. My instinct was to want to rip their masks off like I wanted to mine, but they were permanent. Somehow, in the midst of my pain, sadness, and confusion, their familiarity with mine gave me some sort of comfort knowing that I was not the only one who was different or this way.

Rehabilitation Begins

Finally, the day came for me to leave the burn center and go home. The day that I had dreamed about was really going to happen. Yes, I was really going to go home to see my family! My sister and Mama were coming back. They did love me and had not disappeared from my life!

When I left the hospital, I was covered with all kinds of bandages, splints, and braces. I had to wear a silicone splint on my right hand and another traction splint on my left hand. I also had to wear a face mask and mouth-and-neck brace. I was also required to wear Jobst tights twenty-four hours a day on my arms and legs, along with nasal tubes in both my nostrils in order to keep them open so that I could breathe and to prevent them from closing shut as they healed. My left foot was also fitted with a special shoe to prevent it from getting contractures and turning inward more than it already had.

I was escorted in a wheelchair by a nurse and a Shriners volunteer to the Cincinnati Airport, where I was then flown to Asheville in a small private five-seat airplane. Because Mama did not have her own place, the staff at Social Services made sure that she was provided, in advance, with a new clean apartment that I was to go home to.

I was so excited to get out of the hospital and go to a new home of my own and, most importantly, to see my baby sister again. In all the excitement, I had momentarily forgotten about all the bad things; but most importantly, that I was not the same Teresa that my family once knew. I was different and scary looking now.

When arriving at my new home, Mama hesitantly embraced me, but not the custom hug I had once known. My sister cried in fear when she saw me, turning her back to me and reaching for Mama. And that is when it first started, the sting that would last a lifetime when I felt rejection – in the future and at that very moment it felt like a sharp knife piercing through my heart with overwhelming pain. My sister rejected me. She did not know who I was. How could she not know that it was me, Teresa, her sister - the one that cared about her and loved her and missed her so much? How come she did not know that I was inside of this new body...this mask?

However, like most resilient children, her fear of me subsided and our old bond quickly returned. What also returned was the drinking and neglect - except this time, I wasn't able to fend for Karen or myself. Nothing had changed from before, and we both went long periods without eating, bathing, and, now, my dressing changes. Nonetheless, just like before, Karen and I played as children do, making the best out of the life we were dealt.

I went to the doctor's office every week for checkups. My wounds weren't healing like they should, and I kept getting infections. Mama said that I wouldn't let her change my bandages, and that she could not keep me from playing in the dirt. However, after the sixth week of being home and not getting a good report, Social Services stepped in and decided to remove me from my home because of neglect. It was decided that I would be placed in a special hospital in

Asheville, North Carolina, called the Orthopedic School or Thoms Rehab, where I would go to school, counseling, and occupational and physical therapy.

I was upset about having to leave my family again, but I was promised that they would be able to come visit me once a week in the hospital. Although I had a hard time accepting this, I at least had something to look forward to. I was told that I needed to stay at this hospital so that I could receive the special care that I needed until I got better. So I hung on to the belief that I was going to get better and that things would soon get back to normal. I just needed to hang in there a little longer.

The Orthopedic School and rehab hospital became my home for the next four years of my life. I grew up among other children there who had other physical handicaps, but I was the only one who had been burned. Most of the kids had cerebral palsy or muscular dystrophy. There was also a wing for people who had been in accidents and who were getting therapy to help them recover.

I went to physical and occupational therapy every day. I was taught how to use my hands again and walk properly on my foot, which had to have a splint on it and a special shoe for a long time. It was a slow process, and a very frustrating time in my life. However, I had this incredible determination in me to get out of this place and go home to my family, so I was determined to accomplish everything that was put before me. Of course, I had moments where I wanted to give up. There were days that I walked out of the room or didn't want to do therapy, but over time, I was rehabilitated on how to button my shirt again, zip my pants, pick up things, tie my shoes, feed myself, comb my hair, and dress myself. I literally had to re-learn everything that had once been taught to me as a child. As part of my therapy I even learned to swim and play the piano. This process of being rehabilitated took place every day of my life for the next four years that I lived at the rehab hospital of the Orthopedic School.

Teresa playing the piano

On one occasion when I was in therapy getting a whirlpool treatment, a lady who I didn't know walked in. I was swimming around in the iodine-filled whirlpool bath waiting for my bandages to loosen up and singing "Jesus Loves Me." When she walked in, she asked me who Jesus was, and I shrugged my shoulders and told her that I did not know. It was just a song that I had learned from another child there at the Orthopedic School. To me, there was nothing special about it. It was just a regular song like any other song I knew. This lady quickly corrected me, though, and told me that this song was not just an ordinary song, that it had a very special meaning behind it. She said that it was about a man who loved me very much. This really confused me because there wasn't a special man in my life except my Dad. However, before walking out of the room, she smiled and told me that her name was Mrs. Robinson and that she was going to be my new Kindergarten teacher at school and that she was going to teach me all about this special man very soon.

Mrs. Robinson soon became my kindergarten teacher at the Orthopedic School. The rehab center was an extension of the school. Most of the children that lived at the rehab hospital went to school there as well as children from the outside community. That is how I met my best friend, Sandra. She didn't live at the hospital like I did but rode the little yellow school bus there every morning. I remember the first time she saw me in Mrs. Robinson's classroom. She did not act scared of me; instead, she was curious. "How can she see out of those little holes?" she asked Mrs. Robinson, talking about my eyes. Mrs. Robinson reassured her with a smile that I could see very well.

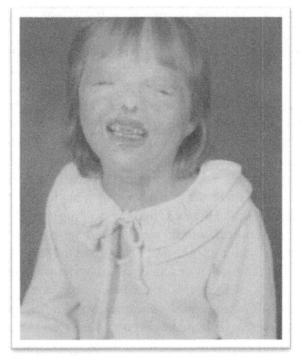

Teresa at the Orthopedic School

Sandra had a beautiful smile and long blonde hair that she kept in pigtails most of the time. She had cerebral palsy and walked on crutches. We quickly became best friends and grew to love each other very dearly while I was at the Orthopedic School. Our bond was so tight that I actually refused to do any of my occupational therapy—such as doing art, playing the piano, or swimming in the pool— without her. We spent so many hours together playing with paper dolls by stringing clothesline across our classroom, making caterpillar houses out of cardboard boxes and saran wrap, being in school plays together, going to camp together, taking turns watering the flowers, feeding the birds, and having crushes on the same boys. I even tried to teach her how to knit using pencils. She said that she loved to watch how my little fingers worked. We also got in trouble together. One time she even helped me cheat on a test. I remember many times being put behind large rolling chalkboards by Mrs. Robinson for having a sassy mouth and Sandra and I trying to sneak and talk through the spaces in the chalkboard. There were so many things that we did together. She really was my best friend, and we knew love spending time together.

Teresa and Sandra doing artwork

I remember every morning excitedly leaving the wing where I lived and walking down the long hallway to meet Sandra and walk to Mrs. Robinson's classroom. Before school started every morning, Mrs. Robinson made us all sit around the table so that she could read us a story. She read different stories from the same blue book that had a picture of a man and children on the front of it. At first, this book, which she called the Bible, was just a bunch of stories to me, which I loved to listen to. But the more she read and talked about this man named Jesus who had died on the cross for our sins, the more I began to love everything about him. As she shared story after story and read to us about how he healed lepers and made blind men see, I began to wonder if this Jesus was really real. Her excitement and love for him made my excitement about him grow. She not only read to us, but she also taught us songs about his life with the disciples, and one of my favorite songs that I remember to this day is about the lepers walking and leaping and praising God.

Her love for this special man made my love for him grow every day, and I soon began to see this man named Jesus as a man who loved me very much. Through her prayers and instructions, I developed a deep connection and longing for him to be a part of my life, and through her help, I asked Jesus to be in my life. Although I did not understand it completely, I soon realized that it was him that had been there standing by my side at the hospital after I got burned, and it was him that had whispered love and hope and determination into my soul to hang on and survive! Although I was only a small child, I quickly developed a deep love and closeness to God. I remember praying very sincere prayers to him, many of them being about my Mama and my baby sister Karen.

As promised, Social Services allowed me to see my Mama once a week, and I was even allowed to go home on the weekends on occasion. I remember crying for days every time I had to leave home and go back to the Orthopedic School. At this point, I did not really understand why Mama could not keep me at home and care for me there. However, over the months, Mama began to not show up for our visits, and they soon began to fade, along with the hope that she would return. However, I continued to believe and to pray every night for her and for the welfare of my baby sister Karen.

Eventually, I was told by my counselor and social worker that I was not allowed to go back home anymore because my Mama was not able to take care of me the way she should. I later learned that I was taken away from my Mama because she was an alcoholic and because of the abuse and neglect. They told me that every time I came back from weekend visits with her, I was filthy, and that she was not taking care of my burns like she was supposed to, and that I always ended up with infections. I was so mad and devastated by their decision. They blamed my Mama for not taking care of me, but in my mind, I blamed myself because I remembered fighting with her about playing outside in the dirt with Karen.

Part of my will to do so well at the hospital was so that I could get better and go back home. I needed my Mama and my baby sister. I needed my family! I was tired of feeling alone in this place. I knew people there cared about me, but they didn't love me like my family did. Everything that I had been working so hard for at the Orthopedic School was suddenly gone! Now not only did I lose my self-image from my burns and my Uncle Clifford from his death in saving me, but I had also lost my Mama and baby sister Karen. What was I supposed to do now? What more was there to work for? What more could I take?

Mrs. Robinson heard about my situation and saw my sorrow. She comforted me whenever I needed it through her constant love, support, and reminders about how I would never be alone with Jesus in my heart. I clung to her reminders every day. *"I am not alone. Jesus is with me. Jesus is helping me. Jesus loves me!"*

With the permission of Social Services, Mrs. Robinson began to take me home with her on occasional weekends. She soon became like a grandmother figure to me. For the first time since my accident, with her involvement in my life, I began to discover a normal life outside of the hospital. Not only did she take me home with her, but she bought me clothes to wear, cut my hair for me, let me play her piano, shared her family with me, and took me to church with her. I remember many happy memories spending the night at her house and playing with her grandchildren on the swing set.

Mr. and Mrs. Robinson

And then there was her husband - Mr. Robinson - whom I came to absolutely love. I remember hanging out with him and helping him work outside and on projects down in their basement. He was such a loving, fun, kind man who I thought was the best buddy in the world to hang out with. I never saw or heard anything but kindness from him. Over the years, I grew to love them both so very much. They played a huge role in my healing process while at the Orthopedic School. I remember thinking that they had to have been sent by Jesus to help take care of me.

Necessary Surgeries

Three times a year, I was flown to Cincinnati, Ohio, for reconstructive surgeries. The Shriners would pick me up from the Orthopedic School, take me to the local airport, and accompany me on a private airplane to Cincinnati. Mr. Bill Norwood, a weatherman from *The Early Morning Show* on WLOS would sometimes take me in his private airplane, along with a nurse from Thoms and a Shriner's volunteer. I used to watch Mr. Bill Norwood's morning show every day, and when he took me, I felt so special to have him as my own personal pilot.

Upon arriving in Cincinnati, the Shriners would then transport me to the hospital to check in. At the beginning of each visit, they would give me a large cotton duffel bag filled with stuffed animals, coloring books and crayons, and other fun things to do during my stay at the hospital, which always consisted of about a week or two because they always did multiple surgeries at one time. This was something that I loved and always looked forward to. It always helped lift my spirits and ease some of the anxiety and fear that I always felt about being alone in this process without any of my family there beside me.

Surgery became a regular part of my life that I could never accept. I feared the process greatly, but I knew that it was a necessary part of my life that I had to endure, at least three times a year.

Getting IVs was definitely my biggest fear because they always had to put them in my right foot the night before my surgery. There was no other place to stick me because of my extensive burns. I remember many times hiding in the bathroom and locking myself in there for hours. I would pray for Jesus to please be with me and to help me get through this again!

I developed anxiety very early on about having surgery. There was no one there to comfort me besides the nurses. It was just me and Jesus. My surgeries became one of the main reminders of why I hated my Mama so much for disappearing and not fighting for me. I prayed for that too. I prayed that I would stop being so mad at her!

The operating room was always so scary. They kept it cold, and it always left me feeling numb on the outside, like I was beginning to feel on the inside. I would pray, "Jesus, please help me do this again" as I was being wheeled into the operating room and laid on a cold stretcher. It was always a frightening experience no matter how many times I had to do it, especially having strangers strapping me down to the metal table. People would come in and out with eyes that I did not recognize and with gowns and masks over their faces that scared me greatly.

Lying there frozen, I would watch them bring packages and put them on silver trays next to my head. I knew there were scary instruments in there that they would use to cut me open, and trying not to think about it made me think about it even more. Next, someone I didn't know would start putting sticky things on my chest, and then I would suddenly be surrounded by beeping sounds. Kind voices behind masks would talk to me and tell me what they were doing before they did it, but their kindness was not enough to keep me from being scared and crying. It would then all end with a mask being put over my face, smelling a horrible smell, and fighting my heavy eyelids to stay open as the light above the table would start spinning me into the dreaded darkness.

I always got sick after surgery and threw up many times. I hated that feeling, but it too was an expected thing after each surgery that I went through. Surgery for me was really hard on many levels. Not only was I alone in the process, but each procedure brought a new physical challenge that involved more risks of infections, more bandages, more pain, more therapy; and the hardest part was acceptance. You see, with each surgery that I went through, a part of me changed physically, and I had to learn to accept that new image of me. I know this is hard for the average person to understand, but after the house fire, my face was unrecognizable. I was a work in progress. My face was like a puzzle that was being rebuilt and pieced back together by the doctors. Who I was becoming was a mystery. Every single time they changed my appearance, I had to re-learn to accept it in the new form that it was. With that always came a feeling of strangeness - much like how I felt in the beginning when I did not recognize who I was.

A Home for Me

The Vandermeers read about me in an article in the newspaper that the Orthopedic School had put out in order that they might find a foster home for me. The article explained that I was a seven-year-old little girl who had been badly burned in a house fire at the age of four, and that they were looking for an adoptive home for me. Betsy said that when she first read the article, she "just started crying." She said that she felt as though the Lord was showing her, her own child. At that time, Jos had just left on an art trip to Europe, and Betsy said that there wasn't any way for her to discuss it with him at that time. She said that she made a deal with God, saying that the only way she would believe that it was meant for them to be my parents was if Jos came home and told her about me and she said that was impossible.

When Jos finally came home, they sat down to have coffee and chat. And then it happened. Betsy said that Jos looked at her and said that there was something that he had to talk to her about later. Betsy said that she wasn't surprised and asked Jos if it was about a little girl named Teresa who lived at the Orthopedic School that was badly burned and in need of a home. As it turned out, a teacher from the hospital at the Orthopedic School had gone on Jos' art study group to Holland, and she had told him about me. They said that they both knew that I was meant to be their daughter from the beginning. They wanted me to come and meet them, but they did not want to force me.

The Vandermeers waited. As it turned out, I did end up meeting the Vandermeers at that time and came and visited them in their home. Here's a letter that my mom wrote to me years later about our first visit:

"Ten years ago, an incredible little seven year old child walked into our house. I was deeply moved as I took her little stubby hand and walked down to the garden with her. This then was Teresa, my little daughter from the heart of Jesus. All through the first weekend, you continued to amaze me. I watched with utter fascination and amusement as you iced the Halloween cupcakes with your little fingers (politely ignoring the knife), "licking" each finger thoroughly before proceeding to the next cupcake. None of us got sick, so we knew that you were a very healthy little child! It was during this icing that you told me about your life: your mother and the little sister still living with her, whom you had great concerns for. Next, you told me about Jesus and how much you loved him. "If I hadn't got burned," you said, "I would not be at the Orthopedic School and I would not know Mrs. Robinson. I am so glad that I got burned, because Jesus loves me very much, and I love Him very much too!" I had to excuse myself. I went to the bathroom to cry. I saw such beauty in you, and it humbled me completely. I was very, very deeply grateful to Jesus that he had chosen me to be your mother..."

The Vandermeers' home wasn't the only one that I visited. However, on this particular visit, I told the social workers that I did not want to live with them because I didn't like their dog! The truth be told, I actually liked Betsy; but in my little girl's mind, I thought that they were too strict and tough on me. While I was visiting there that weekend, they had made me wear my splints, Jobst garments, and the mask on my face; and I wasn't very happy about that. I was looking for a family that would spoil me and be easy on me. Unfortunately, the social workers listened to what I wanted, and the Vandermeers disappeared out of my life as quickly as they had come in.

Betsy and Jos said that they really wanted me to come live with them, but they did not want to force their love on me, so they decided to wait until the timing was right. However, they continued to pray, knowing that God wanted them to be my parents. They knew it from the moment they had heard about me—both on two different sides of the world.

Over the next two years, I visited more homes than I can remember. At first, it seemed fun and exciting. It gave me the chance to leave the walls of the Orthopedic School and get out into the big world. Although my heart was still saddened by the loss of my own family, I embraced the chance to find a new home. The only home I had known for two years now was the Orthopedic School. Mrs. Robinson and the nurses there had taken me under their wing, and the nurses had even nicknamed me Sissy. I had accepted my daily routine there of therapy, school, and roaming the halls reminiscing with other people on the other wings as the way life was supposed to be.

I remember one lady who I had talked to Jesus about so much that she and her husband gave me a

green King James Bible that they had had my name—
Teresa Lundy— engraved on. I still have that Bible
today! Thoms was my home. It was my place of
security. There, at least I had a roof over my head,
clean clothes, and shoes to wear, and my belly was
always full. However, as secure as I felt at Thoms,
there was not ever a day that passed at night when I
went to bed that I did not pray for my real family to
return.

Although the Orthopedic School was a normal part
of my life, in my heart I longed to be loved and to be
part of a real family again, so you can imagine the
excitement that I felt when they told me that they
were going to try to find me a new home. Every
person deserves that, right? However, as the visits to
numerous homes became so many over the next two
years, I began to grow tired and weary by the process.
How hard was it supposed to be to find someone to
love me? I began to feel like a dog being passed
around and tried out from family to family. I always
hoped and prayed that someone would like me and
want me to be a part of their family. The visits never
lasted longer than a weekend, and there are only two
families that I can recall having gone to more than
once. My counselor had told me in therapy that it had
to be the right fit for my needs, and that it might take
time. In my mind, all I needed was a home filled with
happiness and love. How hard could that be to find?

The weekends turned into months, and the months
turned into years. At one time, there was one family
that came into my life that I began to become attached
to. They were an older couple and had one grown
daughter that still lived at home. They lived in

Canton, North Carolina, and they used to pick me up on sporadic weekends and let me stay the night with them and go to their church. They were really kind people, and I was happy during the time that I spent with them. We played in their pool together, we had cookouts, I did makeup with their older daughter, and we even shared one Christmas together. It seemed like they really liked me, and I thought for sure that they were the "right fit" for me.

Over a short time, they did come to love me, and I remember feeling excited about the possibility of them being my new family. But as the process to take me into their home started to be put into place, they quickly discovered that they would not be able to afford the extensive medical costs that I required. With this as a huge barrier, they sadly decided that they wouldn't be able to make me a part of their family. So instead of them remaining in my life, they disappeared, and so did a piece of my heart.

I remember crying a lot over their loss, and I became very angry. With them in my life, I thought that I had a real chance of having a good family and finally being happy. But as it turned out, it did not work out, and all because of my medical needs, which I had no control over. How unfair was that? I was supposed to accept their disappearance in my life and be okay with it, but I wasn't. I missed them dearly, and the happiness that they had temporarily brought into my life.

Social Services worked hard to try to find a home for me, but I was labeled as a difficult case because of my medical needs. As I started to recover more, the reality that I might end up in a group home the rest of my life became a huge possibility.

By age nine, and having lived there for almost four years now, the Orthopedic School no longer was the place that I needed to be, and steps were being taken to come up with other options.

Building Walls

With noticeable changes in my spirit, counseling now became a weekly routine. After four years of being rehabilitated to be self-sufficient, I was tired of fighting any longer. There were too many battles to fight. My hope for a better life was quickly fading, and I found myself no longer wearing just one mask. There were two now. In my childlike mind, I felt as though I had to pretend to be happy despite not feeling that way on the inside. I was quickly learning the ways, not of the big world, but of the real world. I was smart enough to know that no one was going to want an angry, unhappy child to be a part of their family...so I found myself having to pretend to be happy in hopes that someone would want me.

Through the years, with all the disappointments of not being able to find me a home, I dreamed a lot about my real family. I knew that I had already been told all the bad things about my birth mother, but as a child, I really couldn't comprehend why she just couldn't try again. I longed and I prayed for years for her to come back and get me. I even day dreamed about her coming to rescue me and me climbing out the window and us secretly running away together. I wanted to see my sister so badly again that my heart ached with grief. I wanted to talk to her and play with her. I dreamed about how beautiful she would look now all grown up. But through all the years and all my prayers, they never came, and a part of me became very angry. Ella Mae was *my* Mama! She was supposed to fight for me. My memories of her voice and her face faded over the years, and so did my love for her. I hated her for not taking care of me. I hated her for making me have this life in the hospital. I hated her for taking my sister away from me. I could not understand why my life had to be so unfair and why I could not have my Mama back. She was supposed to be there for me. She was supposed to hold me and kiss me when I was scared. She was supposed to protect me from all this craziness. She was supposed to tell me that she loved me and that everything was going to be okay. But she wasn't there. She hadn't been there through any of it. She was long gone, and so was my sister, and I hated her for it.

I never understood why I had to talk to a counselor about the way I was feeling on the inside; after all, no one around me could seem to make it better. I had no choices in my life. I got burned. I had to be taken from my family. I had to undergo surgeries. I had to go to therapy. I had to find a new home and move again. I had to accept whatever was thrown at me, and I knew that no amount of talking about it would change anything. I knew that this was the way that my life had to be now, and that there was nothing that I could do to change any of it. So when the counselors asked me about how I was feeling or how the visits were going, I wouldn't speak. I literally refused to talk to anyone for years about all the bad stuff that I was feeling. I had too much confusion and craziness going on in the inside that there was no way that I could put it into words. It was too much to handle. The only way I knew how to handle life was to shut down and close out the world around me, because I had become angry about everything. Believe me, they tried letting me see different counselors, but none of them could get me to open up to talk. I had become a bratty, strong-willed, stubborn child, and I wasn't going to let the world keep hurting me.

I got to this point because I was so tired of fighting for everything. I was tired of fighting in therapy. I was tired of fighting the pain of all my surgeries, fighting to get used to my hands, fighting to find a family to love me, fighting the anger, fighting the confusion I was feeling inside, fighting the feelings of alienation, fighting and pretending to be happy when all I felt like doing on the inside was bursting from all of the out-of-control things that I could not understand or change. My worldly experiences were shaping who I was becoming, and with all these people that were going in and out of my life and all the disappointments that came with them, I soon became very good at learning to shove the pain down deep within. I began building many walls on the inside. Every pain that I experienced I would shove deeper within.

After a while of doing this, I became very good at it. I became good at quickly forgetting new people's names and faces that came and went in my life - even if they played an important role in my life. I became good at forgetting experiences. I became so good that my past seemed to crumble under me as soon as I took a step forward in a new direction. But most importantly, I became good at being strong and tough and building huge walls and barriers to keep people out. I refused to let anybody else hurt me anymore. I had experienced enough pain. I had become cold hearted and numb on the inside.

My New Family

One day while playing outside on the merry-go-round at Thoms, a social worker came up to me and told me that there was another family who wanted to meet me. I told her that I didn't want to meet anyone new, but before I could say anything else, she told me that they were already there. My excitement and desire to find a new home by this time had completely disappeared. All of the past recurring disappointments had made me lose all hope, so in my mind this time was not going to be any different.

Before I knew it, like a whirlwind, this family had become my new foster home. My new foster mom was an RN and had all the experience and capabilities to care for my needs as a burned child. Because of her training and experience Social Services was hopeful that this placement was going to work. My medical needs had already been discussed, and the finances had been worked out in advance. My foster mom even found me a local surgeon in Asheville, North Carolina, and had me discharged from the Shriners Burn Center in Cincinnati, Ohio, so that I could stay local for all my future surgeries and be closer to home. Big leaps were being taken on everyone's part that was responsible for me to make sure that this placement would work out.

Living in a real home environment quickly proved to be an extreme adjustment and challenge for me. The daily lifestyle and comfort that I had come to know so well in between the safety of the walls of the Orthopedic School, suddenly disappeared. All the familiar routines, nurses, therapists, Mrs. Robinson, and my best friend, Sandra, were suddenly gone.

I was used to roaming the halls of the Orthopedic Hospital doing whatever I liked, watching TV whenever I wanted, never having to follow table rules, never making my bed, never having any chores to do, etc., and now I had to become part of a family unit, and a ton of new rules and responsibilities awaited me. I was not emotionally prepared to handle this, nor did I want to let anyone new into my life. Heck, I didn't even know what a normal family was supposed to be like, because I never had had one, not even as a child. The only thing I knew to do was to quickly tuck away my fears and all my new huge losses and move forward again. I was part of a new family now that expected me to be happy for them giving me a new home. A ton of new experiences awaited me, and I was forced to give this one more try.

My new family lived way out in the country in Leicester on a small farm that consisted of one horse, two goats, four rabbits, a lot of chickens, and a beautiful German shepherd named Elsa. I quickly found out that being a part of a family requires doing chores. Within the first week, I found myself learning how to milk goats, feed rabbits, and gather eggs from the chicken coop.

Teresa feeding the rabbits

I soon discovered that I loved living on a farm. I loved helping take care of the animals and breathing the fresh outside air every day. I had been allowed outside at the Orthopedic School, but nothing like the freedom that I had here. I found myself outside for hours at a time walking down the long dirt roads that surrounded their house, discovering tadpoles in the creeks, playing in a nearby abandoned cabin every day, swinging on the long homemade swing on the top of their mountain, using an outhouse, and even caring for my very own flower garden, which I loved so much. I felt so free here, and life was good. I was happy for the first time in a long time.

Teresa on her swing

My foster family also had four other kids living with them when I came to live there. There was one teenage girl and boy that were real brother and sister to each other and two younger kids that were deaf. Learning to use sign language in their home was necessary in order for the two deaf kids to understand me. I soon found myself learning how to use sign language. I quickly learned how to communicate with them the best that I could with my hands. There never seemed to be a problem with them understanding me, nor I them.

After a lot of new experiences on the farm and

awkwardness in adjusting to their family life, things seemed pretty good. Learning to do chores, making my bed every day, keeping my own side of the room clean, and bathing daily had a certain flow to it that I was able to quickly accomplish. I even found myself starting to open up to my new foster parents, and I soon began to call them Mom and Dad.

In fourth and fifth grades, I had to go to a public school in Marshall, which was a huge, scary experience for me. I would no longer be in a small classroom with a few people with disabilities. For the first time since the fire, I had to be out in the big world around other kids my age who were all normal and less sensitive to my burn scars. I also had to ride the school bus to and from school on my own. There was no one there to shelter me from the cruelty of other kids.

I would like to tell you my memories of this time in my life, but I remember very few. To this day, most of them are buried too deep for me to recall, except for one particular girl named Tanya, who rode the bus with me and became my friend. She is the only person that I remember being nice to me. Even though I was embarrassed about the bald spot on my head, I used to let her braid my hair. She would help me cover it up by pulling both pieces from each side to help hide that area when she braided it. At that time, I also had bad problems with fluid leaking out of one of my ears and watery eyes, and she would always bring tissues to school for me to use on the bus. She was a very kind, thoughtful person, and I remember drawing a picture of a bird and giving it to her as a way to thank her for her friendship and kindness. Besides her friendship, I want to believe that I did not have any bad experiences going to public school at this age, but she has told me otherwise. However, I don't remember any. Any memories other than those with her have been completely wiped out.

Around this time, I remember my foster Mom taking me back to the Orthopedic School because she thought that seeing everyone at my old school would help me with some of my struggles. You would think that I would have been excited to see people I cared for from my past. Sandra, my best friend from the Orthopedic School, says that she remembers when I came back for that visit. She said that I had grown a lot and looked a lot taller. She said that when she finally got the nerve up to ask me if I remembered her, I looked down and shook my head no. She said that it broke her heart! It had only been a year, but I had forgotten my best friend already? That was how good I was at forgetting and blotting my past out. That is what I had learned to do to survive.

Surgery, even while living at my foster home, was a necessary part of my life and something that I had to continue having done several times a year just as before at the Orthopedic Hospital. I remember my foster mom dropping me off at Mission Hospital the night before surgery. That was the custom practice back in the '80s— IVs, needles, surgery tables and masks were still things that I feared greatly, but having to face them alone again was something that I was accustomed to by now. My foster mom said that she wished she could have stayed with me there but that she had four other kids at home to take care of. It became routine for her to leave me alone at the hospital the night before surgery and pick me up whenever the hospital was ready to discharge me.

An Answered Prayer

About a year after living at my new home, I was notified that my younger sister Karen had been placed in a foster home a mile down the road from me. I was told that she had been removed from Mama's house at the age of five after being left alone and found in a nearby ditch. You cannot even imagine the excitement that I felt when I learned that she lived so close to me and that I was allowed to visit her. Jesus had finally listened to me and answered my prayers after all these years!

I was in tears the first time my foster mom took me to see Karen. There in front of me stood my real sister, and she was alive and okay. She was nothing like I remembered her as a baby. She now had beautiful green eyes and curly blonde hair. I knew she did not recognize me either by her hesitance to hug me. I was different than the last time she saw me and I looked different wearing a white face mask.

Teresa and Karen's Reunion

However our bond was strong, and although we had been separated for five years now, we picked right back up where we left off as though our separation had never happened. She never talked about her past, and neither did I. Some things were better left unspoken. However, over the next months, there was not a day that went by, rain or shine, that I did not walk the mile down the long dirt road to see her at her house.

Karen ended up coming to live with me at my foster home. Her foster parents found out that they were expecting a new baby of their own, so Karen needed a new placement. I was beside myself with happiness. I just knew that life could not get any better than this. I was so happy to have my sister back by my side. Everything that I had dreamed about and prayed for all those years had finally come true. All the things that I had loved to do at this home I could now do with my sister. And the bond between us grew stronger and stronger over the next year as we played together, went to school together, and shared family life together. Of course, like all siblings do, we fought and had our arguments; but we made up and went on with life. Our happiness together, however, was short-lived.

Karen and I had been living together almost a year at this foster home when we got a visit from our social worker, Mrs. Meyereich. She told us both that our current foster family did not want either of us to live in their home anymore. Their excuse was that we fought all the time with each other, were very angry kids in general, and difficult to get to know or love. You can imagine the devastation we both felt. I had no idea they felt the way they did about me. I had no idea I was that horrible of a child, and I had no idea that they did not love me in return. I had opened up a piece of my heart again and had grown to love these people in my life the only way I knew how and call them Mom and Dad, and now it all had to end. How could they just throw me away like that after two years of being in their life? Now, not only did Karen and I have to leave our home, but we also had to be separated again. Karen was placed in a home that had always wanted a little girl; and because there was no placement for me at that time, I had to go live in a group home.

One evening, after being in the group home for less than a week, I received a call from Betsy Vandermeer. Even though I had not seen her in almost four years, she told me that their home was still open for me. Betsy said that when the social worker called her and told her about what happened and asked her if she was still interested in providing a home for me, she was filled with excitement and instantly told her yes, even without talking to her husband, Jos, about it first. When Betsy called me at the group home, she asked me if I wanted to come for a visit. At first I said no and hung up the phone. I was grieving the loss of my sister and my other foster parents and I honestly didn't even remember who she was. However, after talking to my social worker about it and her telling me that I would most likely be living in a group home till the age of eighteen because there were no other placements for me I called her back and told her that I would like to come for a visit. That weekend I visited the Vandermeers in their home and at first I did not feel a connection with them, that is, until Betsy started playing the piano and then my spirit lit up. After that we began to talk about their home, money for chores, and the expectations that they would have for me if I came to live with them. Betsy said that she made me go back to the group home after that visit because she felt in her heart that I needed time to think about my decision to be a part of their family. It was important to both her and Jos that I not feel forced into making a quick decision. Betsy said that she dropped me off at the group home after that weekend and went back home.

She said that she was making lunch for her other kids when she got a phone call with a quiet voice on the other end which she recognized as being me. It had only been a few hours since she had dropped me off at the group home, but I told her that I wanted her to come back and get me. Betsy was making lunch at that time for the other kids and she told me that she would come get me later on that afternoon. There was silence on the phone line and then I blurted out, "No! I want you to come get me now!" Betsy said that she chuckled with excitement as her heart lit up realizing that I was finally coming home after four years of waiting for me. She quickly finished up the kids' lunches and came straight over to the group home and picked me up. As it turned out, that day was the day that Jesus brought me back home to my permanent parents - the ones whom He had intended for me to be with four years earlier when my journey to find a home had first begun.

This is a letter that Mrs. Vandermeer wrote to my foster parents about six months after my stay with them:

"I don't know if you knew anything about our previous dealing with Teresa about three years ago. At that time we met and visited with her, but she got scared and didn't want to come—and we felt strongly that we needed to respect her feelings. Though we were very happy to hear that she finally did have a real home, we continued to feel that somehow, our relationship wasn't finished.

Mrs. Edwards knew our feelings, and phoned us immediately when it became apparent that Teresa needed to be moved. We were ecstatic (somehow this seemed like a long pregnancy). Yet again, we felt it was up to Teresa. We now know she has made the right decision. She is doing beautifully integrating beautifully and gracefully with our six other children. Our plans are to adopt Teresa as soon as all the parental ties are severed with you—hopefully by mid-summer. I have a need to deeply thank you for all that you have done for this very special little girl. Due to your wonderful love and care, she's changed from a pretty bratty, strong-willed and rather indulged child into an attractive, outgoing and quite charming young girl. Yes I realize we are still honeymooning - but we're confident that ours will be a lasting parent-child relationship. Only God knows what the future holds, but we're convinced that He brought Teresa truly home."

Betsy and Teresa

The Great American Family

I was not the first foster child that came to live at the Vandermeer home. They had had many other children in their home before me. Jos and Betsy originally had three natural daughters of their own after they immigrated to the States from their native land of Holland. For years, they struggled as a young family while Jos went back to school. Even during their struggles, though, when the Vandermeers were living in a tiny home, they were thinking about adding to their family. They felt that the Lord wanted them to help other children. However, they did not want to go through babies again, so they thought that they would adopt an older child. They did research and found that there were three types of children that desperately needed homes: the physically handicapped, the emotionally disturbed, and the biracial child. The Vandermeers were one of the first families in North Carolina to be approved for biracial adoptions.

The Vandermeers took any child in without seeing them beforehand and without asking any questions about their looks or intelligence. Most of the children who came to live in their home like myself had many emotional problems. The Vandermeers said that much healing always had to take place within their home, but they did not hesitate to seek outside counseling when they thought it would help. They realized that their love could not heal all wounds, but they refused to ever throw anyone out. They said if anyone was to ever leave their home, it would be by their own choice. Jos and Betsy knew that children who came into their foster home had many problems, but they believed that loving these children and helping them was their life's ministry.

The Vandermeers were very strict. They expected any new child who came into their home to learn to fit in with their orderly way of life. They gave every child lots of love, time, chances, and forgiveness. Over a period of two decades, the Vandermeers had taken in over twenty-three children, eight of whom were officially adopted. However, to them, the number of children who came through their home was not important at all; and neither was the child's label, race, or handicap. Their complete commitment to every child was all that mattered to them. The Vandermeers had agreed even before they had started taking in children that whenever a child came into their home, even on a temporary basis, they would love that child as if they were their own from the very beginning. They considered this special gift a true calling from God. Their desire for each child was always adoption. Of course, some children were unable to remain in their home, but Mom and Dad said that they would always remain in their thoughts and daily prayers. Although the Vandermeers' life of service was often difficult and exhausting, it was extremely rewarding. For them, the experience of seeing a wounded and scared child turn around and become an outgoing, healthy, bubbly person surpassed every bit of struggle they ever had to go through.

Because of their service in working with so many children over the years, the Vandermeers were selected by the Family Service Center of Asheville to represent the area in the Great American Families program. One of the criteria for selecting families was on how well they nurtured individual growth, built teamwork, and their service to others in the community. All elements of what a great American family should be.

On June 28, 1984, the family and I were flown to Washington, D.C. In an outdoor ceremony, The First Lady Nancy Reagan, teamed with NBC Weatherman Willard Scott awarded the Vandermeers with The Great American Family Award. Mrs. Reagan told the families, "I know what you have done and the life you've chosen to lead has made you happy, but also, we all know that happiness is never achieved by seeking it. It only comes back to us when we give it to others—and you've given so much."

Nancy Reagan presenting Jos "The Great American Family" Award in Washington, D.C.

Although Mom and Dad were proud of their national recognition, they were both humbled by it. Dad said that there were hundreds of people out there that deserved this award but that they were fortunate enough to have been chosen to represent what others considered an excellent example of what a great American family should be.

Sarah, Theresa, Chris, Tevenia, Kendra, Jos, Betsy, Scott, and Latasha Vandermeer (from left to right, top to bottom)

Mrs. Reagan
requests the pleasure of your company
at the presentation of
The Great American Family Awards
The White House
on Wednesday morning, June 27, 1984
at ten-thirty o'clock

Please Enter Southeast Gate

Please respond to
The Social Secretary
The White House
at your earliest convenience
giving date of birth and social security number
(202) 456-7787

The White House Invitations

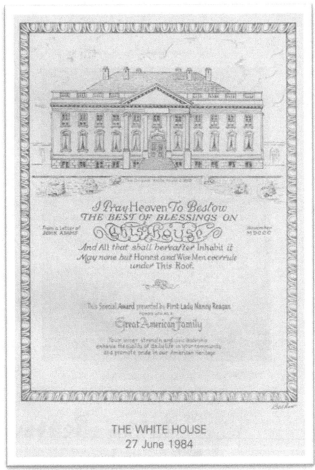

The White House Ceremony Pamphlet

Tough Love

My transition into the Vandermeer home was two months prior to my eleventh birthday. I remember the Vandermeers asking me what I wanted. A bicycle was at the top of my list, but it had to be one without hand brakes so that I could ride it without fingers on my right hand. This would be the first bike in eleven years that I could call my very own. I remember the Vandermeers telling me that normally, they didn't spend more than twenty-five dollars on a birthday gift, but that they were going to make an exception this one time. With that in mind, they took me to Sears to pick out a bike that I liked. You can imagine the excitement that I felt when on my birthday, I received not only a beautiful homemade cake made by my new sister Miriam, but also a beautiful maroon bike and a visit from my real sister Karen, who I found was now living in Leicester.

Teresa and Karen, 11th Birthday party

For the next year of my life, I began to fit into the routine family life at the Vandermeers' home; and Karen was allowed to be a part of my life again. We were allowed to spend occasional weekends together. One weekend, she would come to visit me, and another, I would go to her home in Leicester. Although we could not live together, we were happy being able to talk to each other on the phone during the week and spend weekends together. Our visits together continued for about one year, and then they suddenly stopped without notice.

Karen's family moved to Florida. It happened so quick that I never even got to tell her goodbye. She disappeared out of my life again, and I lost touch with her completely for a long time.

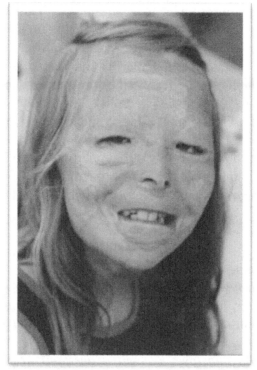

Teresa, 11 years old

During this time, I also spent some weekends visiting my last foster parents at their home. I didn't understand why my visits with them were still allowed once I was removed from their home. I thought they might be able to take me back, and that it could be temporary. I did not know the true reasons why they had made me leave and that this was not a possibility.

Time went by, and even though I grew to care for the Vandermeers very much, I could not tell them "I love you" or call them Mom and Dad because of my continued attachment to my last foster family. They had been my first *real* parents since the fire, and I did not want to let them go. The separation from them left me, yet again, feeling fearful and scared of loving someone new. The fear of the Vandermeers' possible rejection of me was a reality that I knew could happen. Over time, the Vandermeers saw my emotional struggle and realized that if I was to build a parental bond with them, they were going to have to stop all communications with them. Here is the letter my Dad wrote to them about our relationship:

Dear...,

"I hope this letter finds all of your family well and in good health. I do not particularly cherish to write this letter, but I feel the necessity to do so. It pertains to Teresa and her relationship with you. Betsy and I know that you love Teresa very much and we hope that with that love you will understand. We are, as you know, in the process of adopting Teresa and have the full intention to proceed with those plans. In observing Teresa, however, we have noticed, ever since her first visit at your house, that something is blocking her way to adopt us fully as a family, something necessary for an adoption to be successful. Her spirit seems to be divided and torn. Thus after long discussion and prayer, Betsy and I have come to the conclusion that we owe Teresa all the help possible to accomplish that adoption in the heart. It is in our love for Teresa that we are eager to see her whole and healed. Thus we deem it necessary to break ALL contact with you till such a time that

Teresa will live in the reality of having a family of her own. We do not ask her to love you less but help her to bring that love on healthy ground. We know that this decision will be hard on both you and Teresa, but we hope that - for the best long-term interest of Teresa - you will cooperate with this decision. We will keep you in our prayers."

The separation from them left me heartbroken. I did not understand the true reasons why they had chosen to give me up. I still saw them as parental figures, and I still cared for them dearly. As a matter of fact, in my letters to them, I told them that I was praying that they would be able to take me back. This was not because I did not want to be at the Vandermeers but it was because I had a two-year-bond with them that I had not had a chance to develop with the Vandermeers yet. Yes, they were very upset about their decision for us not to see each other anymore, but in reality, they were the ones who chose to let me go in the first place. I too was very angry at the Vandermeers and went through a long grieving process; however, as it turned out, it was the best decision for me at that time.

Adoption Leads to a New Start

Two years after living at the Vandermeers' home, I decided that I was finally ready to be a part of the Vandermeer family and ready to be adopted. Because of my experience at my last foster family and my need to heal from the separation from them, it took me a few years to finally call the Vandermeers Mom and Dad. Being a part of a real family was something that I had dreamed about for years, and to finally now be able to make the final decision to spend the rest of my life with this family, who really loved me, was not only exciting but very scary.

Much to my surprise, with adoption came the option of being able to change my name. The thought of being able to start all over and be called someone completely new was a strange concept to me. Why would I want to do this? For some reason, changing my name did not feel right to me. It was the name that my Mama had given to me, and it was the only constant thing that I had been able to hold on to my entire life. However, at the same time, the idea was intriguing to me. Although I did not want anything to do with my birth mother at this point, I found myself, out of respect for her, not wanting to give up my real name. So I decided to just fancy it up a bit. I remember spending days trying to come up with a better name, but in the end, when signing the final line on my adoption papers, my name didn't change that drastically. It now changed from Teresa Ann Lundy to Theresa Anne Vandermeer.

I would no longer be the old Teresa that everyone

knew. I would now be the new and improved Theresa, with a fresh new identity. The old Teresa, or Sissy, that everyone knew me by would fade away just as my awful past would. I was now given a fresh new start in life. I would be leaving Teresa's old memories far behind and make fresh new ones as Theresa Anne Vandermeer!

Being adopted by the Vandermeers was truly a life changing experience for me in so many ways. Not only did these wonderful people, called by God, decide to take me in and love me as their very own flesh, but they gave me a fresh new start in life. Over the years, they gave me stability and love like I had never known, and they truly saved me from the torment of all the pain and loss that I had had in my past life. Because of their unselfish love and sacrifices for me, I had so much gratitude for them. I could never thank them nor Jesus enough for giving me such a wonderful instant family filled with such incredible people in it. Jesus knew exactly what he was doing when he brought us all together, because much like the Vandermeers love for me as their very own flesh, I too had that same connection with all of them. I never saw any of my brothers and sisters as adopted but, rather, as my real family. Jesus truly could not have picked anyone better for me. Because of their complete acceptance of me, overwhelming love, and daily sacrifices, they helped bring parts of my broken pieces back together.

Life at the Vandermeers' was good but not perfect. Although my parents were very loving, they also were very strict. They had high expectations for all the six kids that were now living in our home, and I constantly found myself struggling on many different levels. One of the biggest things I struggled with greatly was my lack of good communication with them. Because of my tendency to stuff my feelings down deep within, I found myself repeatedly getting upset when my parents tried to verbally discipline or talk to me about anything that I found hard to accept. Not only was I disappointed in myself for not being the best child, but I truly had an extreme fear that they might not want me anymore because of my less-than-perfect actions.

So what did I do? I shut down on the inside because that is the only way I knew how to safely handle the situation. I wanted to be a perfect child - not because they had ever made me feel like I needed to be, but because I did not want to lose them as parents. The fear of me losing this family was tremendous because of my past experiences of loss. The pressure I put on myself was extreme, and the expectations that I had for myself were very high. Everything in my life had been a complete failure and imperfect up to this point, and now all that I wanted was nothing more than for things to finally work out in my life. Failure was not an option for me anymore.

Of course, my resistance to discipline and silence brought about many challenges for my parents. They needed to be able to have me listen to them and be able to correct and discipline me without me running away. So my mom, Betsy, being the creative woman that she was, came up with an awesome solution. She began to write me letters. Her letters would be filled with firm yet loving discipline. She would explain to me exactly what I had done wrong and exactly what she expected from me in the future. She would then put her letters under my room door for me to read in the morning when I woke up. I would then be able to read them in the privacy and comfort of my own room, thereby taking all the time I needed to digest her instructions before facing her for the day.

Needless to say, I did still get upset and uneasy about many things that she wrote to me, but because I was able to digest them on my own, I was able to handle this form of discipline well. Many times I would even reply with a written apology. Verbal apologies were too hard. This form of communication took place all of my teenage years at the Vandermeers' home. Needless to say, I got very good at expressing myself through writing, journaling, and poetry. It became a safe way for me to communicate with my parents, as well as a great way for me to express my inner emotions.

Emotions

Tears, fears, anger, pain
Creeping into her mind again
Sadness, darkness, memories past
How much longer will it all last

Struggling, quarreling with herself
Holding back the tears, she cries for help
Calmness, control, that's what she must do
For her true emotions must not shine through

Deep within, there's a child so full of hate
Not knowing how to face it all, she must escape
Barriers, walls she has many built
Trying to hide all the shame and guilt

Crying out her soul does within
Trying to reach the surface once again
Slowly, patiently the pain is revealed
Maybe in time, she can truly be healed.

During my teenage years at the Vandermeers', I continued undergoing surgeries. By this time, I was able to choose what I felt like I needed to work on or what bothered me the most. I continued to go to the Plastic Surgery Center in Asheville, North Carolina, that my last foster family had set me up with when I lived with them. However, this time, things were so different! I shared with my parents about my past experiences of being alone in Cincinnati and about being alone while living at my last foster home, and my mom Betsy said that it broke her heart. Having grown to love me dearly and share in my fears about being alone during surgeries, my parents decided they would never leave me alone during my surgeries, and they never did. Although they had a household of kids to care for, they both made every effort to make me feel that I was the only one that mattered at that time. They teamed up and came up with the perfect system to help support me through my fears of surgery.

At that time in my life, if you were scheduled to have surgery early in the morning, you had to check into the hospital the afternoon before. Mom would be the one to always take me to the hospital after school and check me into my room. There she would stay with me till I fell asleep that night. We would spend hours playing the game Trouble, Sorry, and Connect Four. I don't ever remember her complaining about how many times we played. All I remember is her being there for me and us laughing our way through the afternoon and evening until I fell asleep and she snuck out to go back home. The following morning, when I awoke, my dad would always be there. He would pray with me, hold my hand as I got my IV started in my foot, and stay with me until the last minute before surgery.

Even though it was not normally allowed, because of my anxiety, the nurses would always allow him to walk with me until I reached the operating doors, where they would then quickly take me inside and immediately sedate me. When I woke up, Mom was always there beside me with her soothing smile to comfort me through my predicted nausea and pain. Also, waiting beside me was a new stuffed animal "friend" to help bring me comfort and to make me smile. Although the surgeries themselves were always scary and painful, my parents always stood by my side. They never failed to show me how much they loved me!

Posttraumatic stress disorder, otherwise known as PTSD, is something that I developed after the house fire. Even though I had tons of therapy up to this point to help me work through some of my fears, I still struggled with a lot of different things in my life. And even though much effort was taken to comfort me through these life experiences, my anxiety still existed. Surgeries were particularly always a big trigger for my PTSD because they were a reminder of what happened to me in the fire. Mom and Dad knew this, which is why they made every effort to help me and comfort me through it all.

There was one surgery that I had as a teen that involved straightening out of my left hand's fingers, in hopes that I might gain better use of that hand since it was the only hand that I could use to grip and pick things up. This surgery involved breaking my bones, straightening them out, and putting two pins in each finger till they healed completely. Unfortunately, several weeks after the surgery, my hand began to throb profusely with pain. Mom took me to the emergency room late that night, only to find out that my left hand had a bone infection in it. X-rays were taken to confirm the infection, and the doctor told Mom that he would have to go ahead and remove several pins that night.

For some reason, the surgeon decided not to use any numbing medicine and pulled the pins straight out. I remember screaming in pain as Mom almost fainted. She said that she was so mad that he didn't use any numbing medicine that she almost cussed that surgeon out right there in the emergency room. After that night, I was put on oral antibiotics, but as it turned out, I ended up having to be admitted back into the hospital later on the following week. Because bone infections are considered very serious, there was fear that I could lose my fingers on my left hand, or that the infection would spread throughout my body. I was put on intravenous medicine; but due to the length of time that I needed to be on medication, it was not financially feasible for me to stay in the hospital. Instead, they got approval from Medicaid for my intravenous medicine to be given to me at home. A central line was put into my neck, and my mom and dad were taught how to give me my half- hour medicine dosages every day through that line.

I was discharged from the hospital, and arrangements were made for me to be able to go to school and still get my medicine. I will never forget the teamwork, selflessness and time that Mom and Dad spent giving me my medicine three times a day.

Dad would he be at my bedside early in the morning before school started with my first dose, he would also meet me at school on his lunch break for my second dose, and then Mom would give me another dose at home before bedtime every night. This went on for over a month till the infection cleared.

Mom and Dad's overabounding love for me showed in so many ways. I remember going through a very hard time in my teenage years with self-image issues. A lot of my friends had boyfriends, and even though I had a lot of good friends, both male and female, I never had a boyfriend. Being a young teenager, I had crushes on boys, but I knew that was all it would ever be. I knew there was no way that anyone would want me to be their girlfriend. The reality hurt, and even though I had accepted the fact that I would probably never have a boyfriend, get married, or have children of my own, I still struggled with wanting to improve my image. I had read about movie stars that had major facial cosmetic surgeries with good results, and I did not understand why a surgeon could not make my face look more attractive. Yes, I had several great surgeons here in Asheville that had helped make a lot of great improvements in many different areas of my body. However, I knew that they were not burn specialists, like the ones I had originally seen in Cincinnati as a child. I needed to talk to a burn specialist to see if they could offer me anything better than what had been done cosmetically on me so far.

I discussed my concerns and desires with Mom and Dad. They knew how important finding out this information meant to me. To my surprise, they scheduled an appointment at the burn center in Boston, Massachusetts. Plans were made for all three of us to take a road trip there to talk to a specialist about possible future surgeries.

The trip to Boston was lots of fun, although I felt very anxious the whole time, anticipating my appointment. I remember eating and walking around the cobblestone streets downtown and feeling very special that Mom and Dad loved me enough to do this for me.

The Boston Burn Center sparked childhood memories from my past, and I recall feeling very uneasy about being there. My appointment did not go the way that I expected it to. The doctor's words quickly turned my anxious excitement into disappointment. I was offered special makeup that could be used on my burn scars, but not any hope for more drastic surgeries. I was told they could fix minor things as needed, but that there was no big surgery that they could offer me that would make a big improvement in my appearance. I left there in tears and without speaking to a makeup specialist. I was silent most of my trip home.

Mom and Dad knew how upset the trip had made me. With the help of my local surgeon in Asheville, they set up a consult with a local makeup artist to teach me how to put on regular makeup. The goal was to help me learn how to use makeup to help cover up some of my scars, and thereby help me with my self-image. I recall Dad taking me to this appointment and spending over $100 in buying Clinique makeup for me.

I went to a Christian private school from fifth to

tenth grades, and then a public school the last two years of my high school. Despite all my emotional problems, I always did well in school and never struggled to make good grades. With the loving support and encouragement of my parents, I was able to participate in a lot of different things that every day normal kids do. I was made to believe that I could do anything despite my disadvantages. As a matter of fact, Philippians 4:13 became my favorite verse when running track and all through the rest of my high school years. I clung to the belief in God's Word that I could do all things through Jesus Christ who gave me strength. If anyone were to tell me that I could not do something because of the way that I was, I would always see that as a challenge and would make sure to prove them wrong. My life story has always been a testament to God's strength in my life. Without Him, I know that I could not have overcome anything.

Throughout my life at the Vandermeers', I won spelling bees, received a reward for exhibiting outstanding Christian traits, was in a public school play, played sports, ran track for years, took ballet and gymnastics, helped start the first literary magazine at North Buncombe High School, took a typing class and (despite my missing fingers) became one of the fastest typists in class, went to my high school prom, and worked three jobs, to name a few. I had a lot of friends and support through it all. Because of Mom and Dad's goals for me to become a strong, independent individual, I did not live a sheltered life.

Through it all, I had a lot of good, meaningful friendships. I always tried not to judge others as I was so often judged. I got along well with most everyone. People seemed to be drawn to me, and as a result, I frequently found myself in the position of giving out advice - even to people I hardly knew.

It was during my first year at North Buncombe High School that a girl on crutches came up to me and asked me if I remembered her, and I told her yes. I remembered her being a girl from my past that used to always wear beautiful sweaters, but I could not recall exactly from where. To my surprise, it was Sandra, my best friend from the Orthopedic School. God had brought our paths back together again! It was not too long after that conversation that I invited Sandra to my house. She brought all the old yearbooks from the Orthopedic School and shared pictures from them with my Mom and me. The pictures helped me to remember the special bond that we had had as children. Because of our similar struggles and connection from the past, we soon became best friends again. We began to spend all our extra time together, including talking on the phone, going to church together, talking about crushes while eating sundaes at McDonald's, hanging out at the skating rink, and working at the Red Cross together, to name just a few. Life's circumstances had separated us once before, but never again. To this day, forty years later I still consider Sandra the best friend I have ever had.

Sandra and Theresa – Best Friends

Although I had what I considered a relatively normal teenage life, I could never escape the reality of my scars no matter how strong I thought I could be. Being in the eyes of the public, I was constantly reminded of being different. For the longest time in my life, I found myself looking down at the ground everywhere I went, only because I could not handle people's reactions to me. The sharp, stabbing pain that I first felt as a young child never seemed to disappear, and neither did the anxiety of meeting someone new or being in the eyes of the public. From the reactions of shock to the looks of pity in their eyes, I was unable to bear any of it. Instead, I stared at the ground and tried to pray and zone out everywhere I went that was outside of my safety zone of people that I already knew. It was a self-defense mechanism that I used to help me get through life.

However, looking down did not always shield me from the pain. People's words often caught me off guard. Many times children asked their parents why I had a mask on, or they told me that I looked like an alien from Mars. I was stared at, pointed at, and even laughed at by both children and adults. One of my worst memories is being laughed at hysterically by an adult that bumped into me at the Asheville Mall one year around Halloween time. I remember being shocked by the adult's reaction to me, and I found myself bursting out in uncontrollable tears as I ran from the mall, knowing that I had scared them. Although people's responses have always taken my breath away, I have been more tolerant of children. But adults should know better! One adult who thought they were trying to be helpful of my situation went so far as to tell me that I should carry a small puppy around with me everywhere I went so that people would be drawn to its cuteness instead of my face.

I have seen fear in parents' eyes for their child as they have intentionally walked another direction just to have their children avoid seeing me. I've witnessed parents ignore their kids questions about me because they were too embarrassed of them or did not know how to respond. I've had people assume that I am mentally challenged, and I have even had people asking my friends beside me what happened to me, as though I could not speak for myself. Because of all these bad experiences in my life at that time, I began to go only to small familiar stores, and I learned to avoid many situations. It even got to the point where I tried to avoid children altogether. If I was to see a child in public or in a checkout line in front of me, I would wait until they were gone or turn my back toward them. I did not want to scare them or have to deal with their responses. A part of me just wanted to become invisible to the world, but my different appearance only made me stand out even more.

Balancing out the good and the bad in my life was a constant struggle of my inner strength, and it was not easy. Not only did I have to deal with these daily struggles, but I still had not completely healed from the scars of my past. Trying to forget or trying to push them down deeper inside does not make them go away—it just compounds them. Certain people, places, or things would trigger a memory from my past, and I would find myself struggling emotionally having to overcome that memory. Many of these struggles were silent or unknown, and I dealt with them by myself. After all, you cannot change reality. You can't change people's insensitivities or the way they treat you. It is what it is, and sometimes the reality of life just plain sucks!

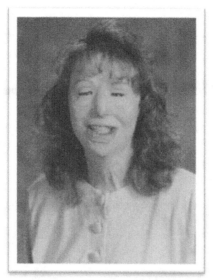

Theresa Sophomore year

I found that running away from my past was not possible, because it always found a way to creep up on me and hurt me. So in the quiet moments of my life, when I could unwind in the safety of my own room, I would pray and journal about my pain. In a moment of strength, I would thank the Lord for helping me to be strong; and in moments of weakness, I contemplated suicide. There was so much inner pain that I felt. I loved the Lord, and I cried out to Him to take me home. At times I felt so weak that I just wanted to give up. Fighting to overcome these battles every day was not worth it. I wanted this lifelong struggle to be over with forever. I loved Jesus tremendously, and I wanted to feel his strong arms around me. I wanted to feel His peace!

The following is an example of letters that I used to write to Jesus as a teenager in pain:

"Father, I am so weak and broken inside. I just want to be in your arms. This world only brings me pain and tears. I don't know how much longer I can hold on. Father, please forgive me for wanting to give up. I'm trying so hard to be strong. But Lord, is this life really worth it? Is this really what you want for your child? I just want to go home I just want all this pain to end I just want to be with you!"

Sandra and Theresa Graduation 1989

Theresa and Mom (Betsy) Graduation 1989

My senior year in high school, I was accepted at Mercy School of Nursing in Charlotte, North Carolina. I was really nervous, but also very excited. I thought that I would make a great nurse because of all that I had personally been through in my life. I also felt that all my experience of being in hospital settings would help me. But my PTSD told me otherwise. I soon found the program anxiety-provoking, and I found myself homesick and wanting to go back home. As it turned out, I only stayed at Mercy School of Nursing for the fall semester of 1989.

I moved back in with my parents, but didn't stay at home long. I ended up getting a job as a CNA at a nursing home and moving into my own place in Leicester, which, coincidentally, was right next door to Sandra's grandmother. I spent a lot of time at her house, talking and hanging out with her. As a matter of fact, she was the first one to introduce me to country biscuits and gravy since I was a child. I remember it very clearly. It was the morning that I picked Sandra up to go to church with me. Needless to say, I spent very little time in church that day; instead, I spent most of my time running back and forth to the bathroom. Having never been exposed to country cooking, the bacon grease went straight through me. That was also the same day that Sandra and I witnessed an old lady in front of us lose her underwear in church. She kindly bent down, picked them up off the floor and stuffed them in her purse like nothing ever happened! Sandra and I could not quit laughing. I don't think either one of us got anything out of church that day. I think we both had to excuse ourselves early from church that day.

That summer, while out in town, I ran into Mrs. Robinson from the Orthopedic School. It was such a shock to see her and her husband again after all those years, and surprisingly, I remembered them. We chatted for a bit, and she gave me her number and told me to stay in touch with her. Consequently, when we met, I was looking for a new place to live. As it turned out, Mrs. Robinson allowed me to temporarily stay in her unoccupied home. Her house was on the market to be sold in West Asheville.

That summer, we spent a lot of time together. She invited me to come over many times and have lunch with her and Travis at their new house in Mars Hill. I have many fond memories of us all sitting on her front porch stringing and breaking pole to pole beans to can while talking about life. That summer she fed me many plates of canned beans, creamed corn, biscuits, and sliced tomatoes from their garden.

Mrs. Robinson and Theresa

Of course, being a retired teacher, Mrs.Robinson wanted to make sure that I went back to college, and stressed to me how important it was for me to get a degree. I really didn't know what my plans for my future were; but getting back into college sounded exciting. That summer Mrs. Robinson helped connect me with the president of Mars Hill College. With his and her help, I was able to get enrolled in school.

That summer I got back in touch with my birth family as well. Somehow I ran into a relative of my birth mother who recognized me. She ended up giving me Mary's number; she was my birth mom's sister. I hesitantly called Mary and ended up going to her house that summer for several visits. My baby sister Melinda was living with her at that time because she could not live with my birth mother. She was eleven. That was the first time that I ever met her.

During one of my conversations with Mary, she asked me if I wanted to see my birth mom, Ella Mae. I was extremely nervous about the visit, but I agreed to meet her there the next time I came to visit. I remember going to Mary's house feeling extremely nervous to see my birth mother. It had been years since I had last seen her. I didn't even remember her voice or her face. It all felt very awkward, and I was unsure how I was going to react seeing her again after all those years. The anticipation almost made me sick. I didn't know if I was doing the right thing. What if I could not handle all the emotions that I would experience?

When I first saw my birth mother, my heartfelt frozen. There she stood in front of me, smiling and with outreached arms; and all I could do was stand there. I didn't know if I was still angry at her after all these years, or happy to see her again. This day that I had dreamed about most of my life was not as I had expected it to be. There was no excitement there at all. This woman was not my mother. She was a total stranger to me. I heard the words "I love you" from her that day, but they meant nothing to me. All I could do was just stand there and smile back, pretending that I was happy to see her again.

That summer, I did end up visiting her several times at her apartment off Tunnel Road, as well as other family members in Tennessee that she took me to visit. It was a strange summer, but a good summer. I learned a lot about her and how she lived. She was a very kind, gentle, loving country woman. I saw many aspects of myself in her that summer and was thankful that God had given me the opportunity to get back in touch with her again. Somehow it felt as though the broken pieces of my life were beginning to come back together. Not only had I gotten back in touch with Mrs. Robinson, but I had also reunited with my birth mother.

Ella Mae, Mindy and Theresa

At the end of summer, I started at Mars Hill College with a major in psychology. I had decided that I was not going to be like my real family - that I was going to make something out of my life. If I graduated, I would be the first person in my real family to get a college degree, and that would be a great accomplishment.

That first year, I lived in the freshman dorm, and it was a lot of fun for me. Although it was a scary experience, I embraced it with much excitement. I made a lot of good friends and formed many meaningful relationships. I recall one day coming out of the dorm and running into someone. I was looking down at the ground, as I was accustomed to doing. This girl said, "Excuse me, may I ask what happened to you?"

I was surprised by her bluntness, but quickly told her that I had been burned in a house fire when I was four. She was the first one who had asked me this question on campus. She told me that she had another friend that had been burned, whom I met shortly after that. Soon after that, we all became very good friends, and we soon all hung out and did things together.

It was cool to know someone else in college that had been burned that I could share stories with and relate to as well as someone who was extremely outgoing that could push me to do new things.

This new friend of mine was a great friend, although she and I were very much the opposite of each other. I was quiet and shy, and she was bold and outgoing; but we complemented each other well. We hung out a lot, and sometimes I would even go home with her on the weekend. On one of the first occasions going home with her, I remember going to the mall. We were in a store looking around, and two old women kept pointing and staring at me. Of course, I saw them, felt the usual sting in my heart, but chose to go on about my business and ignore them.

However, my friend could not do this. It bothered her greatly. She asked me how I could handle people reacting to me that way. I told her that it always stabbed me in the heart but that there was nothing I could do about it. It was part of my life that I had to accept. I could not let it immobilize me or keep me from living my life happily. However, as long as it happened when she was around, she would always put people in their place for being so rude!

No More Pain

College was fun and exciting for me; However, I still struggled with so many things on the inside. Issues from my past still haunted me, and everyday experiences overwhelmed me. Although I had an excellent group of friends that I felt like accepted me, I still felt different on the inside. There were normal things that they were experiencing that I was not, like relationships with guys. All through my high school years and the beginning of college, there were guys that I had crushes on, but I had convinced myself that I would never be able to have a boyfriend or get married or have children. This thought was so hard for me to accept, especially when I saw all my friends around me having relationships. So while I was in college, I began to see the counselor there to talk to her about things.

Her name was Nancy. She was an incredible counselor, and she helped me out tremendously through all my years at Mars Hill College. She was the first counselor that I had ever been able to open up to and talk to about hard stuff from my past. I went to talk to Nancy once or twice a week during my first three years of college. Not only did she help me work through my daily struggles, but she also helped me to feel safe enough to start remembering my past. It was through the comfort of her words and environment that I was able for the first time to begin remembering things that I had shoved down deep inside of me since my childhood. However, because these things were so painful to remember I found myself getting extremely depressed. Facing realities and admitting what I had gone through and the struggles I had been through was emotionally hard.

My Junior year my friend and I moved off campus and got our own apartment together. Coincidentally, we were able to find a tiny little house for rent right down the road from Mrs. Robinson. We moved in together with the help of her parent's right before school started. She lived downstairs, and I lived upstairs. Being her roommate was a lot of fun, but I found myself being alone a lot because she was at class and hanging out with other people. I wasn't surrounded by other people like I had been accustomed to in the dorm setting, and I felt alone a lot. I was still going to counseling with Nancy because of my continuing deep depression, and Nancy ended up referring me to an outside counselor who prescribed me an antidepressant medication. I did not like taking any type of medication and had fears about taking this one. I did not want to take anything that would make me feel out of control or not myself. The mere thought of it gave me anxiety. Most of my life, I had been forced to take so much medication that was out of my control that when given the choice to take this one, I turned it down. However, with Nancy's advice, I agreed to fill it, although I knew in the back of my mind that I was not going to take it.

On several occasions, I found myself at home alone and decided to try out alcohol. I had always promised myself that I would never drink alcohol because of what I went through with my birth mother. I also did not want to drink because I had been told that I was at an increased risk to become an alcoholic because of my genetics. However, out of depression, I decided to try it. The first time I drank, I went through the typical stages of being happy, getting silly, and, of course, throwing up. It was not something that I can say I enjoyed, but I wanted to experience it. It was not long after the first time that I began drinking again.

A part of me liked the way that it made me feel, and at this point, I just wanted to mask all the bad things that I was feeling on the inside. Except this time, when I drank, it wasn't just a few beers. It was multiple ones - seven, to be exact - that I chugged down really fast, which I also mixed with vodka. I did it when I was alone, and on purpose. I was really sad, and I wanted an escape. I wanted to escape so bad that I began to think about ways that I could end my life. My first thought made me think of my depression medication that had been sitting in my drawer, untouched, in my room. I had enough knowledge to know that an upper and a downer was not a good mix. One of my birth brothers had died this way, and at that very moment, that is exactly what I wanted to do.

I wanted to die. I had decided long ago that I had suffered enough pain in this world, and I just wanted it all to be over with. I just wanted to be with Jesus rather than have to deal with the daily struggles of my life anymore. It was not long after those thoughts that I found myself writing a letter of apology to my family and friends. I was very serious about leaving this earth, and I was ready to go. I told everyone that I loved that I was sorry for what I was about to do but that this life was not worth living anymore. I asked them in advance to forgive me. I told them that I just wanted to go home. I wanted this pain to be over with.

After I wrote the letter, I took out my bottle of depression pills and began taking them one by one, until I had taken almost the whole bottle. I lost count after taking twenty-two. After that, all I remember is getting sleepy and lying down on my bedroom floor beside the letter. As I closed my tear-filled eyes, I knew there was no going back because the pills had already been swallowed. I had no fear. Soon my pain would be over with.

Drawing of Jesus by Theresa

Sometime later, my friend came home and found me lying on the floor with the note beside me. I was still awake, but unresponsive. An ambulance was called, and I was taken to the hospital. I remember being asked how many pills I had taken and being told that they were going to have to pump my stomach, and that is exactly what they did. I did not die. My suicide attempt had been unsuccessful.

I was admitted to Highland Hospital after that, which was a mental hospital. I stayed there for about two weeks. It was during my stay there that I worked with an excellent counselor. She helped me to realize that this world owes me nothing, and that my happiness in this life had to come from me and no one else. She helped me realize that I had to love Theresa before I could love anyone else. She helped me to see that I was blaming my unhappiness on others when in fact it was me that was putting myself down and not others.

Others saw me as being strong and an over comer, but I saw myself as being weak and a nobody. She asked me to write a letter to myself, and I did. It was through this letter that I got a new perspective on life. It was through my suicide attempt that my eyes were opened. For the first time since my accident, I was ready to live and be happy.

"Dear Theresa,

What have you done?
Why are you in this dark place locked behind these
walls?
How did you let this happen?
How did you lose control?
You were supposed to be strong.
Do you really want the outside world
To be locked like the inside of your heart?
Do you really hate yourself this much?
What if I want you to love me?
What if I need you to love me?
No one else does so you have to! But wait…
Others do love you.
Your family loves you.
Your friends love you.
But you don't love yourself.
You want to be loved but you won't let anyone in.
You have shut down and you have built walls to keep
people out.
Do you not see this?
Do you not want to face the truth?
You need to stop pretending.
You need to stop fighting yourself
And telling yourself that you are worthless and no
good
Others see the good in you but you turn your back on
them
I want you to see that there is hope
But all you have been able to see is the pain
You keep remembering the past and how it all used to

be
You have to let the pain go now. It is time.
You aren't allowing yourself to be happy
You're dying on the inside, Theresa.
Do you really want to die?
Your time is not over yet.
God is in control of your life not you.
You deserve to live and be happy. Isn't it time?
Time to let it all go
Time to stop shutting out the happiness
Time to stop shoving down the pain
Time to stop being scared to show your emotions
Time to let people see the real you, the pain and all.
Others aren't putting you down,
Theresa, you are
Stop blaming others for your unhappiness.
Don't give up on yourself.
You have something to offer to this world.
You are a child of God's.
You are important.
It's time to leave your past behind.
I know you can't forget about it, but you can forgive.
You can change your future
Will you please try to love yourself?
Life is worth living
Isn't it time to start?"

A Miracle Shall Come to You

Not long after I got out of the hospital, I was invited to go to a revival tent meeting with my birth Mom and her sister. I had no idea what I was getting myself into. It was the first tent meeting that I had ever been to. It started off like a normal church celebration but then ended up being a healing service as well. I remember sitting in my chair feeling very anxious as I sat there listening to the pastor preach.

For some reason, I felt very uneasy. I did not feel uneasy because it was a healing service. I felt uneasy because I knew that I stood out in the crowd as someone who needed obvious healing. As the service went along, I sat there praying to God that he would not come over to where I was seated. Time went by as I listened to this man prophesy and pray for others. Just as the service was about to end and I had let my guard down, I saw him staring at me from a distance.

Before I knew it, he was standing over me with his hand on my shoulder, prophesying over me. I was so nervous that I began to tremble. I don't remember everything he said in the beginning, but when he told me that Satan had tried to take control of my life recently to the point of even trying to take my very own life, I lost it. How could this man possibly know about my recent suicide attempt?

Overwhelming tears filled my whole being. He proceeded to tell me that God had had his hand on me my entire life and that no harm was going to come to me. My time was not over yet. I had a mission to fulfill. He told me that my life was about to change

108

for the better, and that I should be expecting a miracle in my life in the near future. I left there that evening feeling exhausted by all the tears that I had cried, and excited about what miracle he could have possibly been talking about.

My First Love

Two weeks later, after my experience at the tent meeting, I met Rob, the first love of my life. I had gone to the Weaverville Laundromat to catch up on my laundry, and he was there. I remember feeling very uneasy as I noticed this cute guy staring at me. I was used to being stared at, but not by a good-looking man! Before I knew it, he was standing right beside me putting his clothes in the dryer beside mine, striking up a conversation with me. I was so nervous! I could not believe this man—with his piercing blue eyes and charming smile—was actually talking to me.

I don't know what got into me that day, but before I knew it, I was offering him a ride back to his apartment. What in the world was I thinking? The drive was just a short distance down the street, but on the way there, he asked me for my number and said that he wanted to take me out to dinner. I gave him my number and drove off in disbelief knowing that I would probably never hear from or see him again.

To my surprise, a few days later, he called me, and we ended up going out. Not long after that, we ended up getting our own place together; and about four months later, I ended up pregnant with Ariel. That was the beginning of a rocky twelve-year relationship with him. Rob was a very good man, but I soon found out that he was also a very hurt man. He had lost his mother at the age of eleven and had left his father's home at an early age. Because of his struggles in life to get by at an early age, he was forced to grow up

110

fast. As a result, he ended up turning to drugs and alcohol for comfort and became addicted.

On our first date, I had the best intentions to start the relationship out on the right foot, so I asked him outright if he drank or did drugs. I was a Christian girl, and I had been raised to make good decisions. His response was no, only socially, so I believed him. I soon found out, however, that he drank at least a twelve-pack every night, and that when he drank, he became verbally abusive and violent. I was seven months pregnant with Ariel when he first laid his hands on me. I spoke back to him about something, and he shoved me to the ground. He told me to not ever talk back to him again, and I never did. I should have known at that time to get out of the relationship, but he was my first love, and I didn't really think that he meant to hurt me. He apologized to me the next morning, and I accepted his apology. Over the next few years, Rob continued to be verbally and physically abusive to me. I also suspected that he was doing drugs, but I had never found any proof. He was always secretive about how much money he made and was always disappearing to his personal space. One day, determined to find something, I decided to dig through his stuff. To my surprise, I found a bag of something but did not know what it was. I ended up calling Sandra and explaining to her what it looked like. We both decided that it had to be marijuana. Being angry about the discovery and being afraid that it was in my house, I quickly flushed the whole bag down the toilet. Needless to say, I suffered the consequences of that when he got home and discovered that it was missing and that I had just flushed a lot of money down the drain.

I always knew when Rob had been drinking and doing drugs, because he always had that look in his eyes—just like the one you see in the villains in scary movies. I always knew when the abuse was coming. It was like the way people explain knowing they are going to have a seizure. You get that feeling or aura around you. Why I did not leave? I don't know. I think it was out of fear. I did not want to be alone, and he knew this. He played off of my fears. He had me so convinced that no one but him would want to be with someone like me. His exact words were that no one would want to be with a "burnt-up bitch" like me; and unfortunately, I believed him. In the back of my mind, I knew that he was probably right, so I stayed. I thought that life would be better with him than without him.

For years I hid the abuse from everyone, including my family and friends. I just learned to put up with it. I did not want anyone to know that my relationship with him was not perfect. I did this so well that when I finally did seek help people had a hard time believing me. However, as the years went by, the abuse and control grew worse and worse and I ended up confiding in my neighbor. She told me that I could always come to her house if I needed help, and I always kept that escape plan in the back of my mind. I wanted out, I really did, but I did not know how to leave him.

Don't get me wrong, there were aspects of our relationship that were good, which was what I clung to in the bad times. We did go out to eat, to the flea market, and we went on vacations to the beach; but for the most part, he made my existence with him, even during these times, miserable. I had to be the perfect girlfriend, or there would be consequences. He literally tried to control every aspect of my life. He wanted me to stay home, be a mother to our baby, clean the house, do his laundry, and cook for him. He was very jealous of any time that I spent with my friends. He purposely made me spend all my monthly income on our bills at the beginning of the month, and then he would refuse to give me any of his own earnings for gas money or to go hang out with my friends. There were times of desperation when I tried to reach out to family or friends for help, but he would always cut the phone lines so that I could not call out. He was always a step ahead of me. It was no big deal to him because he was an electrician, and it was an easy fix for him when he got home. If there were times that I found a way to get gas money and he knew about it, he would literally pull the distributor cap and wires off of my car so that it would not run, and I would be forced to stay at home all day.

Although I never talked back to him, I did find ways to beat him at his own games, but there were always repercussions, and I knew it in advance. However, living like this for so long, the risks began to outweigh the consequences, and I found myself getting tougher over time.

No matter what, Rob always found a way to get back at me and hurt me on some level. If he could not hurt me verbally or physically, he would hurt me by destroying my cherished personal belongings, and that is exactly what he did on many occasions. I remember one time inheriting a very nice antique coffee table from a friend of my dad's who had died of cancer. I was very proud of having this piece of furniture, and honored that my parents had given it to me. Rob knew this and ended up kicking it and breaking it in half on one of his rages. I cried for days over that loss.

On other rages, he broke glass figurines that he had given me for my birthday or special occasions. One time, he literally turned my whole dish rack of expensive Pfaltzgraff dishes upside down and broke every one of them. He did not care what he did as long as it hurt me somehow. It happened so often that there finally came a time where I quit being excited about getting new things and gave up on trying to have anything nice in my home.

There came a time that I toughened up so much that I was able to escape to my neighbor's after the abuse. The first time I did this was after he came home high. I was sitting on the floor in the living room with Ariel and did not have dinner ready for him. He got mad and started continually kicking me with his steel-toed shoes that left huge instant bruises on my leg. Ariel was there and witnessed it. She started screaming at him to stop. Before I knew it, she had wrapped her body around his legs to make him stop. When he finally did and left the room, we both ran to the neighbors and called the police after taking pictures of the bruises as evidence. You would think at this point that I would have left. It was my perfect opportunity because he was locked behind bars, but I did not. Instead, I cried and felt guilty for having him locked up. I was so stupid, and no matter what he did,

I found a way to post his bond and get him out.

Of course we both honeymooned for a while after these incidents; then his anger would get the best of him again, and the cycle continued. I thought I loved him. He was my first love, and I wanted our relationship to work. I knew the abuse was wrong, but I had had a child with him and did not want to be a single mother, so I prayed for him constantly. I prayed for God to touch his heart and heal him of his anger and addictions. I did not believe that God wanted me to walk out of that relationship, so I kept trying to make it work. I knew Rob believed in God, but he was not a Christian. As a matter of fact, he mocked my faith and Christianity. I remember many times during the abuse praying out loud to God for help, and every time, he would just start laughing hysterically and telling me that God couldn't save me.

The abuse was terrible, but there was more. I remember Sandra telling me that one of her family members saw him at the flea market with another girl. I did not believe her. I knew in my heart that they must have been mistaken. However, I found things on my own that led me to believe that he was being unfaithful to me. I found cigarette butts that were not his in his car, I found college books that someone had left in his car, and I even found a woman's thong shoved under the driver's seat. Even though I did not want to believe it to be true, there was too much evidence to tell me otherwise.

One night, after coming from college, I saw a whole pile of cigarettes that had been dumped out at the top of our driveway. It was the same ultra lights that I had found in his car, which he did not smoke.

When I asked him about it, he said he had no idea what I was talking about. Out of anger, I became brave and began to question him about the other things that I had found over a period of time; and of course, he became furious, and I saw that look in his eyes. He disappeared, and I had this sick feeling that I needed to get out of there immediately, and that was what I tried to do.

With him out of sight, I ran to my car and jumped in to leave; but when I backed up to pull out of the driveway, he reached his hand through the half-rolled-down window and grabbed the steering wheel and keys. It happened so fast I did not even see it coming. Before I knew it, he had thrown my keys in the yard and shoved my head into the floorboard on the passenger's side, leaving me upside down in the car. Before I could even try to get myself up, I found him on top of me repeatedly punching me in the face. The punches happened so many times that I lost count. All I can remember is trying to scream for help, but with each scream, he tried to strangle me. I kept gasping for air. I just knew I was going to die. I don't know if it was from the lack of air or exhaustion, but I just went limp. I could not fight the abuse any longer. I don't know what happened, but he just suddenly stopped, grabbed me up off the floorboard, and swung me out the door onto the ground. He told me to get my ass to bed and that I had better not try to leave him again.

The next morning, I went to my counselor at college, and Rob was arrested. Because of the burns on my face, there was no evidence of any bruises, only my busted lip and the red marks around my neck from him trying to strangle me to death. That was the first time that I ever told my parents about the abuse. I didn't know what to do. I needed somewhere to go. I remember calling my Dad and telling him what happened and asking him to come get me. Both my parents were in shock because they had only known and seen the good side of Rob. It was almost as though they did not believe me, although I knew they did.

Without having money or a way out I went back to him. It was not until years later, when Rob hurt Ariel, who was seven at the time, that I finally said enough is enough. Out of my own stupidity, I had tolerated the abuse for ten years, but in the back of my mind, I had promised myself that if he ever laid a hand on my daughter I would leave him, and it happened. We all were out in town and had stopped at a gas station. Ariel had gone in with her dad to pay. Being a typical child, she wanted a piece of candy, but he told her no. She got upset and started crying in the store. Embarrassed, without thinking, he popped her on the leg really hard and sent her to the car. When she hopped on my lap, I saw that his whole handprint had left a welt on her thigh. I was furious that he had hit her that hard over wanting a piece of candy.

When he came back to the car, instinctively, I yelled at him, and I told him that he better not ever lay a hand on her again. I had talked back to him, and without thinking twice, he backhanded me in the face. It instantly busted my lip, and Ariel's nose, because she was sitting on my lap. Her nose started bleeding profusely, and I grabbed her and ran into the store to get toilet paper. The clerk asked me if we were okay, and I told them no and asked him to call an ambulance. Ariel's nose was bleeding so much I did not know if he had broken it. Before I knew it, the police and the ambulance showed up. Rob was nowhere in sight. He had left the car and ran off on foot. With the EMT's advice, I ended up taking Ariel to the hospital to have her nose x-rayed to make sure that it was not broken.

Of course Social services got involved. That was my breaking point. I was not going to lose my child like my real mother had lost all of us, and especially over an abusive man. Ariel was my saving grace. She was going to save us both from any future abuse. An incident report was written, and I was told that Rob could not be around Ariel for the next six months. Social Services would come out to my house and do random checks to make sure that he was not there and that she was safe. Unfortunately, Rob was there and hiding many times when they showed up, but that was only till I got everything in place so that I could move out, which took me about six months to do. I was determined, for Ariel's sake, to do whatever I could to keep her safe. I now had Social Services on my side, so Rob knew that he could not touch either one of us, or else he would end up in jail.

For the first time in years, I felt freedom that I had forgotten about and was so excited to move out. I did not feel sad. I only felt anger, and that is what helped to push me to do what I needed to do to get out of the nightmare that I had lived in for so long.

After our move, there were times that I did let Rob come around for visits to see Ariel, and there were still moments of weakness that I did sleep with him. I knew it was stupid, but because of his charming ways, I did it anyways. It was during one of these times that I got pregnant with my son, Samuel. Rob and I did not live together, but he chose to be there for the birth of his son. When I finally decided to hold him responsible as a father and filed for child support, he decided to leave. He did not want financial responsibility or anything else to do with raising either one of his children, so he just disappeared out of their lives completely. He moved on to another woman whom he also abused.

Today he owes nearly $100,000 in back child support, but I know that I will never see it. Honestly, I considered his disappearance a blessing. I learned a lot about myself through this relationship but most importantly, I learned what love was and what it was not. I really regret that it took me so long to get out of that abusive relationship, but I am so thankful that I did. A lot of people do not get out alive, and there were times that I didn't think I would either. I know people who have never been through abuse think it is easy to get out of an abusive situation, but I found out otherwise. It took me twelve years to get free. His abusive ways kept me captive, and so did my fears. I had to come to the point where I realized that this abusive relationship was not real love, and it was not worth holding on to. I had to convince and believe in myself that I was a lovable person that deserved respect despite him constantly calling me a worthless "burnt-up bitch."

It was a constant struggle in my mind, but with God's help and strength and the support of family and friends, I was able to release him. I was finally able to come to the point in my mind where even if I was to stay a single mom of two beautiful kids, then that would be better than being in an abusive relationship. But you see, God had other plans for my life. Through all the turmoil, God had allowed Rob to give me two beautiful miracles from this relationship, but my biggest unknown miracle was yet to come just did not know it yet.

And Your Point Is?

Months went by, and I was adjusting well to being a single mom, I had many moments of depression. Being alone was not something that I was used to, and at times, it was very hard. Although I felt an incredible freedom from not being in an abusive relationship anymore, I still missed the companionship.

Fortunately, when I left Rob, I had bought a computer, and I began to explore the online world. It was not long before I began hanging out and talking to people online in chat rooms. At this point, I had no desire to jump into a new relationship. I was just trying to make new friends. Of course, I thought about and prayed for God to send me someone, but I knew I was not ready for that yet, if ever. God, however, had other plans. It had only been two months since Rob and I completely ended our relationship. I was online and had gone into a chat room to look for a person that I had been talking to but did not see, so I left the room - or so I thought I did.

Moments later, I got two messages from two different men. One was a sexual comment, which I completely ignored, and the other was a man who casually said hi and asked me how I was doing. I was completely surprised by his message, because I thought I had left the room already, but I decided to say hi. What first began as casual conversation ended up in planned daily conversations that went on for over two weeks. By this time, I'd begun to realize that we had a lot in common, and that I was beginning to have feelings for him. I wanted to keep talking to him; but at the same time, I did not want to get hurt. I knew that I had to tell him about my burns. I was scared to death to tell him, but it was the right thing to do. I already knew that it would probably end our friendship, but I knew it had to be done. So I told him that there was something that he needed to know about me, and he said, "Okay, well, tell me." So hesitantly I told him that I had been burned as a child and had a lot of physical scars. Without a moment of hesitation, he said, "And your point is?"

I will never forget those words as long as I live! They took me by such surprise that I burst into tears. All I could think about in the back of my mind is what Rob had told me all those years that no one would want a burnt-up bitch like me. I still couldn't believe his casual response, so I went on to tell him more about me. I said that they were really bad and that I had missing fingers.

I didn't think that he really understood the severity of my burns, and I needed him to know without a doubt that they were bad. But my words did not faze him, and again, he said, "And your point is?" I knew right then and there that God had sent this man to me!

After that, we continued to talk every day on messenger, and then eventually began to talk on the phone and through video chat. Our friendship grew stronger over the next few months. One day he called me and told me that he had lost his job as a manager and was really upset. He was going to look for a new job where he was living, but I did not want him to. I wanted him to be closer to me. He lived in North Carolina, about six hours away from where I lived.

After talking about it, we decided that he could move in with me and try to find a job where I lived, and that is exactly what happened. Before I knew it, my sister and I went and picked him up; and he moved in with me. Everything happened so fast, including my pregnancy, which happened almost two weeks after he moved in with me.

Larry was perfect from the very beginning. He was exactly who I had come to know on the Internet and not someone whom he pretended to be. He was loving, genuine, and kind. Our leap in faith to start life together was a very exciting adventure, but also a very scary one, especially for him. He went from being a single man to being an instant stepfather of two kids and another one that would soon be on the way, whom we named Emily Faith. We were two strangers whom God brought together in love, and we both stepped out in faith to start our new relationship together.

Larry had come into my life with open arms and total acceptance of my scars, but he had no idea of the emotional healing that I still had to overcome from my abusive relationship, and neither did I. However, over the years, his kindness, patience, and unconditional love for me proved to be a life-changing experience. Not only did he endure the hard emotional times with me, but he also showed me every single day what true love was all about. There was not one day that Larry did not tell me how beautiful I was to him or show me how much he loved me. His daily steadfast faithfulness to me and never-ending love in my life is the best blessing that I could have ever received from God.

Despite my doubts that I would ever be happy again, and my poor decision-making in the past, God blessed me with the most wonderful man in my life who loves me. I can truly say that God gave me back double for whatever was taken from me in my last relationship. Not only is Larry my best friend, but he truly is the biggest miracle that I could have ever asked for. It took me a long time to heal from my last relationship. Opening up my heart and trusting Larry was not an easy thing for me to do after being in such a long, abusive relationship; however, after nine years of experiencing his beautiful and unwavering love toward me, I was finally able to relinquish my whole self to him completely and give him my heart in marriage. Today we have been happily married for four years, have three beautiful kids, and an incredible relationship built on faith, trust and love.

A Daughter's Forgiveness

Ella Mae, my birth mother, came back into my life in 2012. It had been eleven years since I had last seen her when I was a freshman in college. I had tried to have a relationship with her on and off over the years, but she always found excuses for me not to see her, which really hurt me. Mindy, my youngest sister who was now living with her told me that there was a reason for her avoidance of me. She told me that she "could not stand to look at me because I was a constant reminder of what had happened so many years ago."

Hearing these words coming from my sister about my own mother was heart-wrenching and devastating; and every time I thought about it, I cried. There was nothing that I could do or say to change her feelings about me, so I just had to accept it regardless of how much it made me hurt. This woman was my birth mother, and she was supposed to love me unconditionally and accept me on every level, but she couldn't. She had a second chance to have me in her life as an adult and make things right, but she couldn't handle it. She didn't know how. The only way she knew how to deal with me was through drinking, disappearing, and avoidance; and that is exactly what she did over and over throughout my whole life. Knowing this, all I could do was accept it. I carried that burden of knowledge, pain, and guilt about my scars with me for many years. I knew that what had happened to me, out of no fault of my own, was the reason why my birth mother could not stand to look at me.

This time, however, when she came back into my life, it was by her own free will. For whatever reason, she needed to see me, and I soon found out that it was because she was sick. She told me that the doctors had found a questionable area on her lung when she had received a routine x-ray. After getting a biopsy done, it was confirmed that she had lung cancer. When she came to visit me, she was currently undergoing chemotherapy. She told me that she believed that she could be healed from this and she was praying for God to spare her life. I believe in the power of prayer, and I agreed to stand in faith with her. I also shared my knowledge of using natural remedies that were known to have helped others overcome their bouts with cancer.

On one of her frequent visits to my house, we began to talk about the house fire and what had happened to me as a child. I knew she was praying for healing, I also knew that somewhere in the back of her mind, she feared that she might be dying. I saw that fear in her eyes every time I looked at her. I felt that her visits to me were warranted by the fact that she wanted and needed to release the pain and guilt that she had been carrying about me her whole life. We talked about the fire. We talked about the night it happened. She told me it was not an accident! She told me that the newspaper had said that the fire was started by someone burning nearby tires. The only problem was that people don't burn tires at eleven o'clock at night in the dark. She told me that my birth father, Sammie, had gotten in an argument with a friend of his. His friend had been put in prison for some time. I am unsure if my father was responsible for any of his prison time or not. All I know is that the day after he got out of prison, he had plans to get back at my Father. He came looking for him at my Uncle's house, where I was temporarily staying.

Her talks to me about it were short and brief, as if she could not handle talking about it very long, and I knew this. I also knew that she might be dying and that I needed to know the truth about what happened. I needed closure! I deserved that from her after all these years. I wanted that so bad. I wanted her to make things right. She was the only one who could fit the puzzle pieces together so that it would all make sense. She was the only one who held the key to my heart of forgiveness.

On one of her visits to me while she was sick, her sister Lucille also came. We talked extensively about my accident, and her sister hesitantly agreed to tell me her side of the story. Surprisingly, she was still scared to tell me the truth after all these years, but I was able to persuade her. Apparently, the man who started the house fire was her boyfriend at that time. She told me that the day her boyfriend got out of prison, she was with him. She and another man were with him when he came to my uncle's house looking for my Dad that night. She said it was dark outside, and her boyfriend told her to stay put in the back seat of the car along with the other guy who was with them. He told her that he would be right back. He got out of the car, opened up the trunk, and pulled out something that she said looked like a gas can.

Again, he told her to stay there. The next thing she knew, she saw him running to the car, opening up the trunk to throw something in and then jumping in the car. He told her not to look back as he quickly fled. Of course, her instinct was to look back, and when she turned around, she saw her brother's house in flames. Lucille said that they flew down the road in the car, and as they were driving away, they heard sirens in the distance. She said that she never told the police what happened because she was scared of what her boyfriend might do to her. Instead, she let this man get away with killing her brother and injuring her sister, Ella Mae, and having her sister's daughter almost burned beyond recognition, having had to fight for her life.

I had always known that the house fire was not an accident, but I did not know all of these details. I was in shock. I sat there having to pretend that what I had just heard was okay with me. All I felt like doing on the inside was screaming. How could both my mother and my aunt be a part of this secret that had been hidden for forty years? How could they cover up such a horrendous meditated plan and let this evil man get away? I had no idea that they both knew the truth and decided to stay silent all these years. In my mind, I could not fathom how these two women in my life could hide such a secret. How could they not tell someone about who killed their brother and caused me this lifelong turmoil of pain and suffering? I was angry. I was confused. I was devastated. I was hurt!

And yet here they both were, sitting in my living room, confessing all this to me. What was I supposed to do with this information? They needed to tell someone! It wasn't too late! They could do something about this! I could do something about this! This man could finally be imprisoned for his wrongdoings.

Justice could be brought about even after forty years. I sat there frozen. I thought there had to be a way to get them to tell the police. It wasn't too late. Lucille told me she still had a relationship with this man. She knew where he was. I knew I could do something about this. They both had just confessed everything to me. I had just heard it myself. They were key witnesses to a murder.

My birth mother, Ella Mae, admitted to me that she knew that he started the fire. She told me that he was a very dangerous man and that she had been too scared all these years to tell anyone. She said that she was scared for her life. That is why she never told anyone. That is why she kept it a secret for so long.

After talking to Ella Mae and Lucille for a very long time and pleading with them to tell their story, they both finally agreed to meet with a detective at the Asheville Police Department. I told them that I would make an appointment and let them know when it was. My birth mother agreed to come back from Tennessee for the appointment.

I contacted Detective Elkins at the Asheville Police Department. I made an appointment and went up there in person to talk to him. I told him about my accident and told him that I had two key witnesses that were willing to come forward and testify against this man. After listening to me ramble on, he looked at me with interest and told me that this case concerning this man was actually a cold case that they had been trying to solve for many years. Apparently, this man who had been involved in the fire was also believed to be involved in the death of another African American man. He was also the main suspect in the death of my oldest sister, Linda. She had been murdered. She was eight months pregnant at the time. Her body had been tied to the back of a car and dragged down the road. They found her body on the road, along with her dead baby who was found outside of her womb, a few feet away from her.

Detective Elkins told me that even though they believed this man was responsible for all these murders, to this day, they had never been able to get enough evidence against him to take him to trial. I was optimistic at this point. If I could get Ella Mae and Lucille to testify against him, justice could finally be served.

Ella Mae, Lucille and Mindy met me at the Asheville Police Department to talk to the detectives about what they knew. Lucille was taken to one room to talk to a detective, and Ella Mae and I were taken into another. I sat there in that room staring at the walls, listening to Ella Mae as she admitted for the very first time in forty years what had happened and who was responsible. She explained to the detective that she had been unable to tell anybody because she was afraid that he would kill her. When asked if she knew anything about the African American man, she said yes. She said that she saw this man's bloody shirt and wallet at her house. She said that this man and several others took the African American man up into the woods. She believed that he had been set on fire alive. Although she claimed to not be involved, she stated that she heard them talk about it and was witness to his personal belongings. She stated the man's correct name when asked. She also said that she believed he had killed Linda over a jealousy issue over another man. I sat there in awe as the detective wrote everything down. What I witnessed hearing in that room was like something from a murder movie. How could any of this be true? How could one man kill so many people and get away with it? How could he still be out there? There was no telling what else he had gotten away with over the years. I suddenly became afraid that by me reopening this cold case, this man would come after me again. Lucille now knew where I lived, and she still talked to him. I quickly became fearful that this man would try to come after me, but this time, actually succeed in killing me. I was so full of anxiety and began to wonder if I should have done this? I spent months being scared to sleep. I was afraid that I was going to wake up with my house on fire again. I needed to move! I no longer felt safe.

Detective Elkins and I talked several times on the phone after that. I told him about my fears. He informed me that they had surveillance on this man's house. To comfort me, he told me that this man now lived in South Carolina. After a month of surveillance, they were able to get permission to interview him and give him a lie detector test. Detective Elkins told me that "he failed it royally." However, he told me that lie detector tests do not hold up in court. He also told me that because all these things happened thirty to forty years ago, they had absolutely no physical evidence to try him on.

Detective Elkins also told me that if they took him to trial without having any physical evidence, there was a great possibility that he could still get away with everything, and that if they did find any new evidence in the future, they would not be able to try him again. Needless to say, my heart was broken by this news. All I wanted was for this man to finally be charged and for justice to be served. I wanted it for me, my sister, and the African American man that he killed.

However, I had to trust Detective Elkins's advice and let it go. To this day, I have never heard anything further from him about the cold case.

Of course I was angry for a short time over not being able to do anything about this man, and it seemed so unfair. It seemed unfair to know who did this to me; it seemed unfair that the secret became known and nothing could be done about it. It seemed unfair that there was lack of evidence; but most importantly, it seemed unfair that this man got away with multiple murders and caused me a lifetime of suffering. In my despair, I cried out to God. I knew that He was in control of it all, and it was through my prayers I realized that this man would have to answer to God one day, and I also realized that my un-forgiveness of my past had to finally be released. I was not doing myself any good by holding on to something that was out of my control. I had to give it to Jesus.

Over the next eight months, God began to soften my heart as I slowly watched Ella Mae's health fade. For the first time since childhood, I was able to really open up my heart to love her again as a daughter. It was not because she was my birth mother, as I had always told myself, but because she was a child of God's. Despite all that she had put me through throughout my life, God helped me to see what a beautiful person she was on the inside. Once again, I saw her big heart and felt her kindness and love for the Lord. Most importantly, Ella Mae finally came forward and did the right thing for me.

Even though justice wasn't served in court, it was in my heart. What I had needed all my life from her as my birth mother was finally given to me. She showed me love, and she tried to make things right at the very end. For the first time since childhood, I was able to tell her that I loved her and really mean it. For the first time, I was able to respect her. For the first time, I was able to tell her "thank you for coming forward." And most importantly, I was able to find peace in my heart to forgive her. You see, it might have taken her forty years to make things right, but she did it, and because of it, my heart was finally able to let go of my past and truly be healed.

Ella Mae visited me a few more times during her illness, but the cancer finally got the best of her to the point where she became bedridden. Before long, her breathing became labored, she quit eating, and she was put on hospice care. My sister Karen, who lived out of state, and I went to visit her in Tennessee toward the end of her journey. She was so happy to have all three of her girls with her again. She did not want us to leave. We laughed with her, we comforted her, and we prayed with her. During one of our conversations with her, my birth mother said that she saw angels in her room. We all knew that she was nearing death. At one point, when I was alone with her in the room, I whispered in her ear not to be scared, and that it was okay for her to let go. Karen had to leave to go back home, and my birth mother asked for me to stay, but I couldn't. I had to get home to my family. I told her I would come back on Friday. I knew it my heart when I left that it would probably be the last time I saw her alive.

A few days later, Mindy called me and told me that she was close to death. I knew I needed to go see her, but I did not want to be there when she died. I knew I could not handle it. Friday came, and I had plans to go see her. That afternoon, before leaving, I got a call from Mindy telling me that Ella Mae had taken her last breath.

Her funeral and burial was at a little white country church on Union Chapel Road in Weaverville, North Carolina, where the rest of our family is buried. It is also the same road where my Uncle's house was set on fire with me in it. Since that day, I have never returned to her gravesite, and I never will. Her memory will forever live in my heart, but that chapter in my life is now closed. The pain and the torment that I have endured all these years has been buried along with her. Through the grace of God, my heart has finally been healed. Although I will never understand why I had to go through everything that I did, I know that God had a purpose in all of it. If my life story can be an inspiration of courage and strength to others who have gone through any type of suffering in their life, then I know that my purpose here on earth has been fulfilled.

Karen, Theresa, Mindy (sisters)
and Ella Mae

From Suffering to Blessings

Throughout my life, I have endured a lot of pain, loss, and suffering. There were many times that I wondered how a loving, merciful God could have allowed me to go through so many accounts of suffering and turmoil in my life. There were many times, through my own weaknesses, that I became angered by my situations and, at one point, even tried to end my own life. Through all of it, I found myself asking God why; and sometimes I even wondered if it was something that I had done to deserve it.

However, over time, I realized that no one is exempt from suffering in this lifetime. Most everyone has some sort of trial that they have to overcome. Unfortunately, mine were many. I was born into a dysfunctional, alcoholic family; was burned in a house fire; lost my self-image, my uncle, and almost my own life. I was taken from my birth parents, lived in a hospital setting for four years, endured over a hundred surgeries, went through multiple foster homes, tried to commit suicide, endured a twelve-year-long abusive relationship, and on top of all that still, I continually have to deal with the daily pain and suffering of just being different in such a cruel world.

Many people and circumstances failed me throughout the majority of my life, and I realized that I could not get through it alone, so I drew closer to God. I found myself having to become completely dependent on Him to help pull me through. I cried out to Him many times, and I also clung to His Word in Philippians 4:13 which states "I can do all things through Christ who strengthens me." God became my hope and strength, to keep moving me forward, and to not give up. Over the years, He built me up from the inside out. He continually sharpened my character and helped me to persevere. Through every situation that I had to go through, He shaped and molded me into His own image and made me spiritually stronger.

In the Bible, in the book of John, Jesus is asked by a Rabbi why a man was allowed to suffer. Jesus replied, "It was in order that the works of God might be displayed in Him." I truly believe that God did not cause all of my pain and suffering, but that He did allow it. I also believe that there was a purpose in all of it and that God used it for the manifestation of His Glory.

God is a merciful God, and although He allowed me to suffer through many hardships throughout my life, He also gave me many blessings. All along the way, He had His hand on my life. Through every trial that I went through, He took care of me. Most importantly, He brought special people into my life to share my pain and joys with such people as my sister Karen; my teacher Mrs. Robinson; my lifelong best friend, Sandra; my adoptive parents the Vandermeers; my loving and faithful husband, Larry; my three beautiful children - Ariel, Samuel, and Emily; my Granddaughter Khloey and all of the other supportive and meaningful friendships that I have had throughout my lifetime.

My prayer is that my personal story of hardship, perseverance in Christ and His blessings in my life will be an example for others to live by. God never promised us a life free of suffering, but He did promise us that He would be there through all of it.

He is in control of everything, and if we will just allow Him to hold our hand through it all, we will overcome any battle set before us.

What are you going through today? What battles are you fighting? You can either get angry at God and fight against your struggles, or you can choose to keep a positive mind-set and grow closer to God through all of it. Just remember that you are not alone! God loves you and has your best interest at heart. He is a loving Father and is there for you to call upon at any time. He promises in His Word that He will not allow anyone to go through more than they can bear. What will your decision be? Will you take His hand today and let Him walk with you through your life? Or will you become bitter and deny His presence in your life? The decision is yours!

I saw Him work many times in my own life and I know that if I would have never gone *through the fire* or anything else that I had to that I would not be the strong person that I am today. There is no telling how my life would have turned out or where I would be in life's journey. My prayer for you right now is that God will touch your life immensely and that you too will be open to see His presence in every aspect of your own life. Start learning today to lift God higher through all of your battles and in every area of your life, and He too will bring you Through the Fire!

"When you go through deep waters, I will be with you. When you go through rivers of difficulty, you will not drown. When you walk through the fire of oppression, you will not be burned up; the flames will not consume you." (Isaiah 43:2)

Made in the USA
Columbia, SC
06 April 2020